YOU CAN SPEAK

notionpress.com

YOU CAN SPEAK

CHITRA

notionpress.com

Notion Press

Old No. 38, New No. 6

McNichols Road, Chetpet

Chennai - 600 031

First Published by Notion Press 2016

ISBN 978-93-5206-543-1

This book is dedicated to my dear daughter

Dr. Bharati Vasant Lunge Patil,

M.B.B.S., D.A. (PUNE).

Contents

Preface

The chief motive behind preparing this book is to enable any person to speak English fluently provided he or she is minimum 10th pass or 12th pass. It will be much better if he or she is a graduate or a post graduate in any faculty.

Simply passing these exams will not make a person good at speaking fluently. Some additional efforts are necessary to be good at speaking fluently in English. One has to follow certain practical guidelines to develop the art of fluency in spoken English.

Herein, more stress is laid on loud reading, learning new words, writing the positive, negative, interrogative and interrogative negative sentences and reading the recommended books.

If these are practiced daily, minimum for a certain time, the success is assured within a short period of time. Read this book seriously. It should not be read as a novel which is read once and kept aside. It is advisable to read it, practicing the suggestions sincerely for better results.

I wish the reader a grand success in acquiring the art of spoken English.

– Chitra

Foreword (Asian)

English speaking has become very much essential for dealing with people in different walks of life. It may be law, medicine, engineering, commerce or any other faculty. If proper efforts are put in, one will acquire the art of spoken English.

The proper efforts are explained by the author. Anybody who has passed 10th, 12th, graduation and post graduation can speak fluently with the help of this book. It should be studied and practiced seriously to attain the desired results.

I recommend this book for learning to speak English fluently without any reservation.

Dr. Vasant R. Lunge Patil,
M.B.B.S., M.D. (Community Medicine),
Professor, PSM, PDM Medical College, Amravati,
Joint Secretary, Indian Medical Association,
Maharashtra State
President Dodge Ball Association, Maharashtra State,
President, Bharat Krushak Samaj, Amravati District.

Foreword (Europian)

Since last three decades, I am in Gulf countries, holding different important positions in oil and gas industry. My position demands for daily meetings with various people of different departments. I have to question the concerned people for information.

I have come across many people from non-English speaking countries like India, Pakistan, Bangladesh, Nepal, Sri Lanka, Philippines, Thailand, Indonesia, etc. I have observed these people speaking poor English. Majority of them cannot speak properly. They cannot express their thoughts effectively.

I have gone through the book YOU CAN SPEAK written by CHITRA of India. It is written in a plain English language. It can be clearly understood by any person with matriculation and above qualification. As has been suggested by the author, practice is necessary to acquire the art of speaking. The book is very useful to learn spoken English.

Without any reservations, I recommend the book to all persons from non-English speaking countries for reading and practicing to learn spoken English. No doubt, the reader will be able to express his or her thoughts in English more clearly.

– ANTHONY DEKKER,

General Manager,

Weir Arabian Metals Company L.L.C., Al-Khobar,

KINGDOM OF SAUDI ARABIA.

Acknowledgement

I express my deep felt thanks to the writers of following books for the treasure of information received to present this book on spoken English.

- Oxford Advanced Learners Dictionary
- Oxford English Language Reference Books
- Cambridge Phrasal Verbs
- Little Oxford Thesaurus
- Oxford English Minidictionary

Introduction

Who doesn't like to impress others by his or her speaking? Who doesn't want to be a fluent speaker? Of course, everybody wants it but how many are ready to put in the proper efforts to achieve the fine art of fluent speaking? Nothing is possible without the input of systematic efforts!

You speak to express your thoughts and feelings. You can express your feelings by using different words and phrases. If you use proper words in proper situations, the meaning will be clearly understood by the listener. The different situations are discussing, explaining, convincing, persuading, arguing, etc. Similarly, you have to use proper words in different moods like happy, unhappy, satisfied, dissatisfied, angry, etc. If you use difficult words, your listener will not understand and the process of communication fails. You have to use simple words and talk in a simple way to make others understand you.

I came across many people who were not able to speak fluently. Some of them were struggling to speak. They were struggling because of lack of sufficient vocabulary. Many of them could not speak because of fear of criticism. They were worried because people may laugh at them. I have observed this drawback in many people. Very few were found to have good vocabulary and command.

I have made an honest effort to enable people who are interested in speaking fluently. English is a foreign language and we are not speaking it right from birth. A child in English speaking country starts to speak English first and write next. Right from birth to school going age, the English child communicates with family members in English language. A child in Asian nation communicates with family members in its mother tongue or any language other than English. Learning English language starts later. This is the basic difference. In convent schools in India, they teach from nursery but in non-convent schools they teach from eighth standard. Naturally, it becomes difficult for students whose parents do not know English. They cannot guide them in the homework of students. This is the reason many of our children do not pick up English. A fear is generated in the minds of majority of people about the English subject. Naturally it leads to poor performance.

Here, I have concentrated on spoken English only. I have attempted to make it useful to learners from non-English speaking countries. If you desire to learn how to speak fluently, I assure you it is not difficult. For learning to speak fluently, it is necessary to do a little bit of writing and loud reading. Loud reading helps to speak fluently. Proper guidance is required to reach the destination. You have to put in proper efforts to learn anything. Similarly, here also serious efforts are necessary. There is no short cut to success. Success demands organized and consistent efforts.

You can speak fluently by increasing your vocabulary. The meaning of vocabulary is the "list of words with their meanings". You have to increase your word power. Understand the meanings of different words. How to increase the word power? Keep the Oxford English dictionary handy. Refer to it to know the meaning of words. Go for simple words and know their meanings. People understand simple English. Do not use high sounding words because many people do not understand them. The main purpose of communication is to make others understand your point of view, your opinion, and feelings of happiness, unhappiness, anger, sorrow, satisfaction, etc. You will start speaking fluently in a short period of time. To tell you plainly, do not expect miracles. Simply wishing to speak English will not help. You have to decide to speak English and follow certain guidelines given below. Please remember, consistency is necessary to achieve success in any field.

To learn to speak fluently, you have to spare 90 minutes daily for first three months.

Take a text book of English subject of eighth or ninth class or take the English newspaper. **Read the editorial column 'loudly' for 30 minutes**. Please note the word 'loudly'. Loud reading is recommended to train your tongue. This is called gymnastics of tongue. The loud reading is necessary to make your tongue accustomed to English words. Your tongue must have practice daily. Practice it for 30 minutes. You are speaking your mother tongue fluently because your tongue is accustomed to it since your birth. Now you are learning a foreign language that is English. The English words are new to your tongue. Therefore, it is advisable to read loudly. Please take care to keep the level of sound to yourself and not disturb others.

Everyday learn minimum 10 to 12 new words.

Take a notebook, write a word, see the meaning of it, write down the meaning of it and utter it loudly ten times. **Make it a practice to write down 10 to 12 new words**. If you do more than 12 words, it is well and good. Your progress will be fast. Minimum 10 to 12 words per day will give you around 1000 words at the end of three months. To begin with, this is enough but do not stop here. Make it a regular practice. This is how you will add these words to your memory. In this way, you can go up to any number of words. For speaking fluently, 2000 words are sufficient. There are more than 250000 words in English. One cannot master all these words. Therefore try to know 2000 common words. Further progress depends on you. More words you learn, more fluently you will speak. It has to be fixed in your mind to increase word power. It has to be fixed in your mind to increase the word power. This will take 30 minutes, totalling to 60 minutes.

How to select 10 to 12 words daily?

It is very simple. Take any English newspaper. Go to the editorial column. Copy the editorial column, about 20 lines. Here you will get the practice of writing also. After writing the page, read it loudly. While reading you will come across some words whose meaning you do not know. You underline the word by a red pen. Then write down the words one below the other. Take an Oxford English dictionary. Search for the meaning of each word and write down the meaning. Say the words loudly and their meanings. Do it minimum 10 times. **Loud reading and repetition is a must**. Thus you will go on adding to your vocabulary. Your tongue will have practice to speak English words. This will take your 30 minutes, thus completing your 90 minutes of the day.

Books recommended for speaking fluently.

You will make it a regular practice to read the books. The books of following authors are the best for beginners.

1. Earl Stanley Gardener

2. James Hadley Chase

3. Dale Carnegie

These are very simple in language. You will understand the words and sentences easily. These books are small in size and light in weight. You can easily carry them with you. First time, you may understand less than 50% of the book. Read next book, you will understand 75% of it. Read the third book, you will understand 100% of it and you will be extremely happy. Thus you will develop the liking and you will not stop. They are cheap also; may be Rs.90/- per book. They are easily available at any book stall. The more you read, the more you will like to read. Your vocabulary will go on enlarging. This will increase your confidence while speaking. You will gradually find that you are making progress. You begin with the book written by Earl Stanley Gardener. You will find it very interesting. There are different situations, court scenes, crime scenes and so on. While reading, study how the sentences are made, how the questions are asked and how they are answered. Study how the situations are narrated. You will come to know the use of words, use of phrases.

It has to be noted that the written English is different from the spoken English. The following sentence is the example of written English. Such sentences are printed in the book and we understand it by reading once or twice. The following sentence is the example of written English. You will not be able to use such a long sentence while speaking. You will not remember all the words and your listener also will not be able to understand. Read the following sentence carefully.

On one fine morning, he saw an attractive girl, young, tall, slim, clad in yellow sari, with a shopping basket in hand, approaching the bus stop to catch a city bus for going to market.

Written English is edited many times before printing. It is not advisable to use such a long sentence while speaking. You have to speak in small sentences. The above sentence is to be split into small sentences. Just observe how it is spoken.

It was a fine morning.

He saw a girl.

The girl was young.

She was attractive.

She was tall.

She was slim.

She wore a yellow sari.

She was holding a shopping basket.

She was walking to a bus stop.

She was going to catch a city bus.

She was going to market.

Observe carefully how a long sentence is split into a number of small sentences. You can see which is easy to speak and understand. It is easy to speak in small sentences using simple words. In high school, you were taught written English. You try to speak written English and hence you find it difficult. Do not imitate the written English in text books. Try to speak in small sentences. In the beginning you speak in small sentences. After getting the grip over the subject, you can go for compound and complex sentences.

There are a couple of TV channels showing English movies daily. Listen to the spoken English in films. See the English movie whenever you happen to sit before the TV.

Your main aim is to speak fluently. For that it is not necessary to be perfect in grammar. However, you have to keep some basic things in your mind.

In each tense, there are four types of sentences. They are **positive, negative, interrogative and interrogative negative sentences**. It is essential to know these sentences. They will be useful to narrate the happenings. They will help to ask questions. It is desirable to learn asking questions of different kinds. For your practice, plenty of questions are given in the questions chapter. Concentrate on questions and you will be a good speaker. It will take few weeks to be thorough with the types of sentences. Once they are understood, your progress will be noticeable. I once again stress on the fact that you need not be an expert in grammar. Do not be scared by the grammar. The example is given below to show four types of sentences.

Simple present tense:

I go to market.	- Positive sentence
I do not go to market.	- Negative sentence
Do I go to market?	- Interrogative sentence
Do I not go to market?	- Interrogative negative sentence

Likewise, four types of sentences are formed in each tense.

A basic thing you have to know is the difference between written English and spoken English. When you write, you get as much time as you want for thinking about the subject matter. You have got sufficient time for planning the construction of sentences. You have enough time for choosing the right words and phrases. You have enough time for doing the corrections and editing.

But when you speak, you don't have time to do all these activities. The entire planning, correction, editing, etc. have to be done in a short limited time. You have to do all these things in your mind as you speak. Quite often, you don't remember the right word and you hesitate. There will be the silence of a few seconds. If you stand silently without speaking for a few seconds, it looks awkward. Here, you can use the **hesitation fillers** to fill the gap. The hesitation fillers like **'well', 'yes', 'no', 'I mean', 'you know', 'you see'**, can be used while speaking. The hesitation filler **'you know'** is most frequently used while speaking.

See the examples below:

I have got too much to – **you know** – I am a little busy today.

What do you think of – **you know** – he may not agree with us.

What's this about – **I mean** – is he going to resign?

He was not asking me to – **well** – I don't want to tell you.

Whenever you don't remember the proper word, you can use the hesitation filler and choose another sentence to continue your talk. There is nothing wrong in using the hesitation fillers. It is the standard practice to use the fillers. While speaking, the use of hesitation fillers is accepted. You will not be able to speak right from the first day. Make it a firm rule to speak to your friends and family members in English.

No matter, you may speak wrongly. Only that person commits mistake who tries to speak. Refer to the book, correct the mistake and continue to speak.

Another important aspect to be discussed is the **fear of criticism**. You have to take out the fear of criticism from your mind. You are afraid that people may laugh at you. You are afraid that you may be exposed before people. This is the fear of criticism. Remove this fear from your mind. It is very easy to criticize and laugh at others. The people who laugh at you are non-doers. They cannot achieve anything positive. You have to just neglect them.

Begin with determination and spare 90 minutes daily for learning to speak English fluently. A day will dawn, when the same people will admire your speaking. This time will come within three months provided you work systematically. You have to work hard. There is no magic wand for learning English. Remember to read the sentences loudly. You must read loudly to train your tongue and it is most important.

Now you are holding in your hand a book of practical knowledge. It is not a novel which is read for entertainment. The value of a novel is zero after its reading is over. It is kept on the shelf and forgotten. This book is not like that. You read it quite often and follow the suggestions. Please read it loudly wherever suggested. You will certainly be benefitted. The success comes to those who act. Action is important. Simply wishing will not help. Remember, investment in time and effort will surely pay. Do not believe that paying tuition fees at a teaching centre will magically give you the ability to speak fluent English.

After a few months, you may start using phrasal verbs in your speech. The phrasal verbs are phrases that have verbs in them. They are made up of verbs followed by words like: **out, in, up, off, down, across, through, away, with, for, forward, forth, around, back, about, etc.**

For example, take the core verbs such as: **take, look, sit, stand, come, go, fill, move, keep, put, check, etc.** The **phrasal verbs** are formed as shown below.

Take back = if something takes you back, it makes you remember a period or event in the past

That piece of music **takes** me **back** to my childhood.

Take up = to start doing a particular job or activity

Have you ever thought of **taking up** acting?

Look out = to search for and find something

I will **look out** the recipe and send it to you.

Look for = to try to find something or someone, either because you have lost them or because you need them

How long have you been **looking for** a job?

It's no good **sitting around** the house all day doing nothing.

Stand over = to stand close to someone in order to watch what they are doing

His mother **stood over** him while he finished his homework.

Stand for = if a letter stands for a name or a word, it is used to represent it

UFO **stands for** Unidentified Flying Object.

You may refer to Cambridge Phrasal Verbs dictionary. It is available at a nearby book stall.

To begin with, speak in active voice. It is easier to speak in **active voice**. See the following example.

Do it at once. - It is in active voice.

Let it be done at once. – It is in passive voice.

You can see four words are needed in active voice and six words are needed in passive voice. The meaning of both sentences is same. **Do it at once** is much easier to speak than **Let it be done at once.**

Few more examples are shown below. Observe them carefully.

Do not gamble.	- Active voice
You are advised not to gamble.	- Passive voice
Stand up on the bench.	- Active
You are ordered to stand up on the bench.	- Passive
Please help the poor.	- Active
You are requested to help the poor.	- Passive
He can win the prize.	- Active
The prize can be won by him.	- Passive

You can see it is easier to speak in passive voice.

Now the practice is necessary and it is you who has to put in maximum efforts to achieve success in the art of speaking English fluently. Remember the proverb, "Slow and steady wins the race". If you take positive steps, a grand success is assured. You will be able to speak English fluently in three months.

Make it your dream and you reach your goal. Play steadily to reach the destination.

I will be the happiest person on the earth if you use this book and be a fluent speaker. I pray the Almighty to give you enough patience and perseverance to reach your goal.

Wishing you all the best!

Elementary Grammar

Grammar is the science of organizing the usage of language. English grammar is about the detail knowledge of the usage of English language.

Words

Letters make words. There are 26 alphabets; 5 vowels and 21 consonants. These letters make words like – stand, sleep, work, drink, eat, run, play, sit, etc.

Phrases

A phrase is a group of words and this group does not make complete sense. A phrase comprises a single element in a sentence. A phrase represents an idea. The words in a phrase are closely related to each other. The phrase acts as a whole in the sentence.

Following are the examples of phrases which are shown in italics.

The sun sets *in the west.*

He found a pencil *on the table.*

The soldier found a knife *with bloodstains on it.*

She saw a cat *sleeping on the roof.*

Having obtained my father's permission, I went to Delhi.

Sentences

A sentence is a group of words making a complete sense. Note the following group of words.

The cat is sleeping.

Get away from here.

Flowers bloom in the rainy season.

Who is she?

What are you doing?

Clauses

A clause is a sentence that is part of a larger sentence.

Example:

My brother helped me *when I was in trouble.*

He informed me *that he wanted money.*

The dog started barking *when it saw a thief.*

She laughed at him *when he jumped from a wall.*

In the above sentences, the portion in italics is a subordinate clause and the rest portion is principal clause.

Parts of Speech

There are EIGHT (8) divisions of words according to their positions and usage in sentences. They are called Parts of speech. They are given below.

The Noun

The Adjective

The Pronoun

The Verb

The Adverb

The Preposition

The Conjunction

The Interjection

The Noun

The name of a person, place or a thing is called a noun. The noun is a naming word.

Example: table, book, Germany, song, player, chair, pen, cupboard, bench, etc.

The Adjective

An adjective is a word that qualifies a noun. It is something 'added to' the noun.

Example: *colourful* flower, *smart* boy, *black* board, *white* chalk, etc.

The words *colourful, smart, black* and *white* are used to describe the nouns flower, boy, board and chalk.

The Pronoun

A pronoun is a word which is used in the place of a noun.

Example: Kamala is going to market. She is going for shopping.

The word 'she' is the pronoun. It is used in the place of Kamala.

The Verb

The verb is a word that describes an action.

Example: You eat an apple. The word 'eat' is the verb.

I read a letter. The word 'read' is the verb.

run, cut, sleep, stand, talk, play, fight, etc. are verbs.

The Adverb

An adverb is a word that adds more information about place, time, manner, cause or degree to a verb, an adjective, a phrase or another adverb.

Example: 'speak *kindly*', '*incredibly* deep', '*just* in time', '*too* quickly'

'kindly', 'incredibly', 'just', 'too' are all adverbs.

The preposition

It is a word or group of words, such as *in, from, to, out of, on behalf of, after, at,* used before a noun or pronoun to show place, position, time or method.

Example:

The dog is *in* the garden. * I come *from* school. * You go *to* market. * He spoke *on behalf of* me. * She went *to* school *after* breakfast. * I sleep *at* night.

The conjunction

The conjunctions are words used to connect words, phrases, clauses or sentences.

Example: pencil *and* rubber, table *and* chair

The window was open *and* he was sleeping.

She is beautiful *but* impolite.

You select this *or* that ball.

The interjection

It is a word or sound to express sudden feelings or emotions.

Example:

Alas! She is gone!

Oh! What a pity!

Ugh! What a dirty place!

Masculine and Feminine Nouns

Masculine	Feminine	Masculine	Feminine
father	mother	gentleman	lady
son	daughter	husband	wife
brother	sister	man	woman
boy	girl	king	queen
bachelor	spinster	monk	nun
cock	hen	sir	madam
dog	bitch	uncle	aunt
bull	cow	nephew	niece
drone	bee	wizard	witch
stag	hind	drake	duck
lion	lioness	author	authoress
priest	priestess	patron	patroness
host	hostess	master	mistress
actor	actress	emperor	empress
conductor	conductress	hero	heroine
shepherd	shepherdess	songster	songstress

Masculine	Feminine
executor	executrix
steward	stewardess
manager	manageress
instructor	instructress
man-servant	maid-servant
he-goat	she-goat

land-lord	land-lady
milk-man	milk-woman
bull-calf	cow-calf

Formation of Plurals

singular	**plural**	**singular**	**plural**
boy	boys	cat	cats
girl	girls	dog	dogs
hero	heroes	echo	echoes
mango	mangoes	buffalo	buffaloes
potato	potatoes	torch	torches
watch	watches	ditch	ditches
class	classes	tax	taxes
kiss	kisses	box	boxes
photo	photos	piano	pianos
dynamo	dynamos	ratio	ratios
story	stories	storey	stories
army	armies	lady	ladies
baby	babies	city	cities
pony	ponies	life	lives
knife	knives	calf	calves
wife	wives	thief	thieves
loaf	loaves	leaf	leaves
shelf	shelves	wolf	wolves
hoof	hoofs	roof	roofs
dwarf	dwarfs	man	men

foot	feet	goose	geese
mouse	mice	louse	lice
ox	oxen	child	children
crisis	crises	basis	bases
index	indices	radius	radii
formula	formulae	terminus	termini
analysis	analyses	criterion	criteria
daughter	daughters	sister	sisters

Three Main Tenses and Twelve Sub-tenses

Three main tenses

1. Present tense
2. Past tense
3. Future tense

Each main tense is having four sub-tenses and they are:

Present tense

1. Simple present tense
2. Present continuous tense
3. Present perfect tense
4. Present perfect continuous tense

Past tense

1. Simple past tense
2. Past continuous tense
3. Past perfect tense
4. Past perfect continuous tense

Future tense

1. Simple future tense
2. Future continuous tense

3. Future perfect tense
4. Future perfect continuous tense

Types of sentences

In each sub-tense, there are four types of sentences and they are:

1. Positive sentences
2. Negative sentences
3. Interrogative sentences
4. Interrogative negative sentences

In each sub-tense, the above mentioned four types of sentences are given for practice of writing with different verbs and loud reading. Following is the example of sentences using the verb **'sleep'** in **simple present tense.**

I sleep.	We sleep
You sleep	You sleep.
He sleeps	
She sleeps	They sleep.
It sleeps	

Let us write down four types of sentences from each of the above sentences

Positive sentences:

I sleep. * We sleep. * You sleep. * He sleeps. * She sleeps. * It sleeps. * They sleep.

Negative sentences:

I do not sleep. * We do not sleep. * He does not sleep. * She does not sleep. * It does not sleep. * They do not sleep.

Interrogative sentences:

Do I sleep? * Do we sleep? * Do you sleep? * Does he sleep? * Does she sleep? * Does it sleep? * Do they sleep?

Interrogative negative sentences:

Do I not sleep? * Do we not sleep? * Do you not sleep? * Does he not sleep? * Does she not sleep? * Does it not sleep? * Do they not sleep?

You will make it a practice to write these sentences using different verbs in different tenses. All the sentences in different tenses are shown below for your study. Observe carefully and write down four types of sentences using different verb daily. **This is the basic foundation and you have to attend to it daily for gaining confidence.**

PRESENT TENSE:

1. Simple Present tense
2. Present Continuous tense
3. Present Perfect tense
4. Present Perfect Continuous tense.

1. Simple Present tense

Positive sentences:

I go. * We go. * You go. * He goes. * She goes. * It goes. * They go.

I see a man on the tree. * I think he is right. * That man climbs up the ladder. * My sister teaches in a school. * He works in a big company. * The school opens next week. * She cooks food. * He watches television. * I wake up early in the morning. * It rains heavily.

Negative sentences:

I do not go. * We do not go. * You do not go. * He does not go. * She does not go. * It does not go. * They do not go.

I do not see a man on the tree. * I do not think he is right. * That man does not climb up the ladder. * My sister does not teach in a school. * He does not work in a big company. * The school does not open next week. * She does not cook food. * He does not watch television. * I do not wake up early. * It does not rain heavily.

Interrogative sentences:

Do I go? * Do we go? * Do you go? * Does he go? * Does she go? * Does it go? * Do they go?

Do I see a man on the tree? * Do I think he is right? * Does that man climb up the ladder? * Does my sister teach in a school? * Does he work in a big company? * Does the school open next week? * Does she cook food? * Does he watch television? * Do I wake up early? * Does it rain heavily?

Interrogative negative sentences:

Do I not go? * Do we not go? * Do you not go? * Does he not go? * Does she not go? * Does it not go? * Do they not go?

Do I not see a man on the tree? * Do I not think he is right? * Does that man not climb up the ladder? * Does my sister not teach in a school? * Does he not work in a big company? * Does the school not open next week? * Does she not cook food? * Does he not watch the television? * Do I not wake up early? * Does it not rain heavily?

2. Present Continuous tense

Positive sentences

I am going. * We are going. * You are going. * They are going. * He is going. * She is going. * It is going.

I am playing hockey. * She is buying vegetables. * He is scolding his son. * It is raining heavily. * We are watching television. * You are working hard. * They are playing golf. * I am running to catch the train. * We are meeting to discuss. * You are eating a banana. * Policeman is controlling the traffic. * We are going to market. * Dog is chasing the cat.

Negative sentences

I am not going. * We are not going. * You are not going. * He is not going. * She is not going. * It is not going. * They are not going.

I am not playing hockey. * She is not buying vegetables. * He is not scolding his son. * It is not raining heavily. * We are not watching television. * You are not working hard. * They are not playing golf. * I am not running to catch the train. * We are not meeting to discuss. * You are not eating a banana. * Policeman is not controlling the traffic. * We are not going to market.

Interrogative sentences

Am I going? * Are we going? * Are you going? * Are they going? * Is he going? * Is she going? * Is it going? * Are they going?

Am I playing hockey? * Is she buying vegetables? * Is he scolding his son? * Is it raining? * Are we watching television? * Are you working hard? * Are they playing golf? * Am I running to catch the train? * Are we meeting to discuss? * Are you eating a banana? * Is the policeman controlling the traffic?

Interrogative negative sentences

Am I not going? * Are we not going? * Are you not going? * Is he not going? * Is it not going? * Are they not going?

Am I not playing hockey? * Is she not buying vegetables? * Is he not scolding his son? * Is it not raining? * Are we not watching television? * Are you not working hard? * Are they not playing golf? * Am I not running to catch the train? * Are we not meeting to discuss? * Are you not eating a banana? * Is the policeman not controlling the traffic?

3. Present Perfect tense

Positive sentences

I have played. * We have played. * You have played. * He has played. * She has played. * It has played. *

They have played. * I have just arrived from school. * You have promised me a treat. * We have given our consent.* He has fought with a strong man. * She has lived in Kanpur for six years. * It (dog) has run for a long time. * They have seen the aquarium. * I have spoken to her about my paper. * We have hunted a ferocious tiger. * She has loved him heartily. * I have cleaned the car.

Negative sentences

I have not played. * We have not played. * You have not played. * He has not played. * She has not played. * It has not played. * They have not played.

I have not yet arrived from school. * You have not promised me a treat. * We have not given our consent.

* He has not fought with a strong man. * She has not lived in Kanpur for six years. * It (dog) has not run for a long time. * They have not seen the aquarium. * I have not spoken to her about my paper. * We have not hunted a ferocious tiger. * She has not loved him heartily. * I have not cleaned the car.

Interrogative sentences

Have I played? * Have we played? * Have you played? * Have they played? * Has he played? * Has she played? * Has it played?

Have I just arrived from school? * Have you promised me a treat? * Have we given our consent? * Has he fought with a strong man? * Has she lived in Kanpur for six years? * Has it run for a long time? * Have they seen the aquarium? * Have I spoken to her about my paper? * Have we hunted a ferocious tiger? * Has she loved him heartily? * Have I cleaned the car?

Interrogative negative sentences

Have I not played? * Have we not played? * Have you not played? * Have they not played? * Has he not played? * Has she not played? * Has it not played?

Have I not yet arrived from school? * Have you not promised me a treat? * Have we not given our consent? * Has he not fought with a strong man? * Has she not lived in Kanpur for six years? * Has it not run for a long time? * Have they not seen the aquarium? * Have I not spoken to her about my paper? * Have we not hunted a ferocious tiger? * Has she not loved him heartily? * Have I not cleaned the car?

4. Present Perfect Continuous tense

Positive sentences:

I have been playing. * We have been playing. * You have been playing. * They have been playing. * He has been playing. * She has been playing. * It has been playing.

I have been living here since 2004. * The dog has been sitting here for one hour. * He has been swimming for one hour. * He has been playing tennis for two hours. * I have been doing my homework since Sunday. * It has been drizzling since last four hours.

Negative sentences:

I have not been playing. * We have not been playing. * You have not been playing. * They have not been playing. * He has not been playing. * She has not been playing. * It has not been playing.

I have not been living here since 2004. * The dog has not been sitting here for one hour. * He has not been swimming for one hour. * He has not been playing tennis for two hours. * I have not been doing my homework since Sunday. * It has not been drizzling since last four hours.

Interrogative sentences:

Have I been playing? * Have we been playing? * Have you been playing? * Has he been playing? * Has she been playing? * Has it been playing? * Have they been playing?

Have I been living here since 2004? * Has the dog been sitting here for one hour? * Has he been swimming for one hour? * Has he been playing tennis for two hours? * Have I been doing my homework since Sunday? * Has it been drizzling since last four hours?

Interrogative negative sentences:

Have I not been playing? * Have we not been playing? * Have you not been playing? * Has he not been playing? * Has she not been playing? * Has it not been playing? * Have they not been playing?

Have you not been living here since 2004? * Has the dog not been sleeping here for one hour? * Has he not been swimming for one hour? * Has he not been playing tennis for two hours? * Have I not been doing my homework since Sunday? * Has it not been drizzling since last four hours?

We have completed writing the sentences in PRESENT TENSE along with its four sub-tenses. Now let us write down the present, past and past participle of all verbs therein.

Regular Verbs:

Put either 'd' or 'ed' at the end to make past and past participle tense. This is applicable to all **Regular Verbs.**

Regular verbs are shown in present tense, past tense and in past participle tense.climb-climbed-climbed, work-worked-worked, open-opened-opened, cook-cooked-cooked, watch-watched-watched, rain-rained-rained, scold-scolded-scolded,control-controlled-controlled,chase-chased-chased, hunt-hunted-hunted, discuss-discussed-discussed, clean-cleaned-cleaned, love-loved-loved, arrive-arrived-arrived, promise-promised-promised, drizzle-drizzled-drizzled,

Irregular Verbs are shown below. teach-taught-taught, swim-swam-swum, do-did-done, wake-woke-woken, see-saw-seen, think-thought-thought, catch-caught-caught, eat-ate-eaten, buy-bought-bought, run-ran-run, meet-met-met, speak-spoke-spoken, fight-fought-fought, give-gave-given.

Observe the meaning of following words and use them in your speech suitably.

'to work' is a verb and 'work' is a noun.

He is *working* in the garage. [verb]

I am still looking for *work*. [noun]

'to cook' is a verb and 'cook' is a noun.

Where did you learn to *cook*? [verb]

She was employed as a *cook* in a hotel. [noun]

'to rain' is a verb and 'rain' is a noun.

It was *raining* heavily. [verb]

Don't go out in the *rain*. [noun]

She *watched* the kids playing in the yard. [verb]

My *watch* is not running. [noun]

Now we will write down the sentences in the past tense.

PAST TENSE

1. Simple past tense
2. Past continuous tense
3. Past perfect tense
4. Past perfect continuous tense

1. SIMPLE PAST TENSE

Positive sentences:

I went. * We went. * You went. * They went. * He went. * She went. * It went.

I went home last night. * We cooked the food ourselves. * You performed well in the examination. * You dug a deep well in your compound. * He drank milk yesterday evening. * He worked for the full day. * She danced very well. * It rained heavily in the city. * They slept in the tents during the camp. * It barked at a stranger. * I saw her last Sunday.

Negative sentences:

I did not go. * We did not go. * You did not go. * They did not go. * He did not go. * She did not go. * It did not go.

I did not go home last night. * We did not cook the food ourselves. * You did not perform well in the examination. * You did not dig a deep well in your compound. * He did not drink milk yesterday evening. * He did not work for the full day. * She did not dance very well. * It did not rain heavily in the city. * They did not sleep in tents during the camp. * It did not bark at a stranger. * I did not see her last Sunday.

Interrogative sentences:

Did I go? * Did we go? * Did you go? * Did they go? * Did he go? * Did she go? * Did it go?

Did I go home last night? * Did we cook the food ourselves? * Did you perform well in the examination? * Did you dig a deep well in your compound? * Did he drink milk yesterday evening? * Did he work for the full day? * Did she dance very well? * Did it rain heavily in the city? * Did they sleep in tents during the camp? * Did it bark at a stranger? * Did I see her last Sunday?

Interrogative negative sentences:

Did I not go? * Did we not go? * Did you not go? * Did they not go? * Did he not go? * Did she not go? * Did it not go?

Did I not go home last night? * Did we not cook the food ourselves? * Did you not perform well in the examination? * Did you not dig a deep well in your compound? * Did he not drink milk yesterday evening? * Did he not work for the full day? * Did she not dance very well? * Did it not rain heavily in the city? * Did they not sleep in tents during the camp? * Did it not bark at a stranger? * Did I not see her last Sunday?

2. PAST CONTINUOUS TENSE

Positive sentences:

I was going. * We were going. * You were going. * They were going. * He was going. * She was going. * It was going.

I was playing tennis with her. * We were watching television. * She was reading when her mother called her. * He was walking across the road. * It was raining heavily. * You were running to catch the bus. * The dog was barking at him. * She was buying vegetables. * I was swimming in the pond.

Negative sentences:

I was not playing tennis with her. * We were not watching television. * She was not reading when her mother called her. * He was not walking across the road. * It was not raining heavily. * You were not running to catch the bus. * The dog was not barking at him. * She was not buying vegetables. * I was not swimming in the pond.

Interrogative sentences:

Was I going? * Were we going? * Were you going? * Were they going? * Was he going? * Was she going? * Was it going?

Was I playing tennis with her? * Were we watching television? * Was she reading when her mother called her? * Was he walking across the road? * Was it raining heavily? * Were you running to catch the bus? * Was the dog barking at him? * Was she buying vegetables? * Was I swimming in the pond?

Interrogative negative sentences:

Was I not going? * Were we not going? * Were you not going? * Were they not going? * Was he not going? * Was she not going? * Was it not going?

Was I not playing tennis with her? * Were we not watching television? * Was she not reading when her mother called her? * Was he not walking across the road? * Was it not raining heavily? * Were you not running to catch the bus? * Was the dog not barking at him? * Was she not buying vegetables? * Was I not swimming in the pond?

3. PAST PERFECT TENSE

Positive sentences:

I had gone. * We had gone. * You had gone. * They had gone. * He had gone. * She had gone. * It had gone.

I had gone to market for buying a shirt. * I had invited him for dinner. * We had requested them to attend the function. * You had scolded the boy for his misconduct. * He had escaped unhurt in the severe accident. * She had answered to all your questions. * It had rained before I reached there. * They had arrived to attend funeral ceremony. * They had lived in the city since a long time. * I had helped him when he was studying in university.

Negative sentences:

I had not gone. * We had not gone. * You had not gone. * They had not gone. * He had not gone. * She had not gone. * It had not gone.

I had not gone to market for buying a shirt. * I had not invited him for dinner. * We had not requested them to attend the function. * You had not scolded the boy for his misconduct. * He had not escaped unhurt in the severe accident. * She had not answered to all your questions. * It had not reached before I went there. * They had not arrived to attend the funeral ceremony. * They had not lived in the city since a long time. * I had not helped him when he was studying in university.

Interrogative sentences:

Had I gone? * Had we gone? * Had you gone? * Had they gone? * Had he gone? * Had she gone? * Had it gone?

Had I gone to market to buy a shirt? * Had I invited him for dinner? * Had we requested them to attend the function? * Had you scolded the boy for his misconduct? * Had he escaped unhurt in the severe accident? * Had she answered to all your questions? * Had it rained before I reached there? * Had they come to attend the funeral ceremony? * Had they lived in that city for a long time? * Had I helped him when he was studying in university?

Interrogative negative sentences:

Had I not gone? * Had we not gone? * Had you not gone? * Had they not gone? * Had he not gone? * Had she not gone? * Had it not gone?

Had I not gone to market to buy a shirt? * Had I not invited him for dinner? * Had we not requested them to attend the function? * Had you not scolded the boy for his misconduct? * Had he not escaped unhurt in the severe accident? * Had she not answered to all your questions? * Had it not rained before I reached there? * Had they not come to attend the funeral ceremony? * Had they not lived in that city for a long time? * Had I not helped him when he was studying in university?

4. PAST PERFECT CONTINUOUS TENSE

Positive sentence:

I had been going. * We had been going. * You had been going. * They had been going. * He had been going. * She had been going. * It had been going.

I had been working in post office for four years. * We had been practising golf since Monday. * You had been working in a multinational company. * He had been playing chess for four hours. * They had been polishing the floor. * She had been sitting on the chair since morning. * It had been raining heavily since morning. * My keychain had been stolen by somebody. * The washing machine had been used extensively.

Negative sentences:

I had not been going. * We had not been going. * You had not been going. * They had not been going. * He had not been going. * She had not been going. * It had not been going.

I had not been working in the post office for four years. * We had not been practising golf since Monday. * You had not been working in a multinational company. * He had not been playing chess for four hours. * They had not been polishing the floor. * She had not been sitting on the chair since morning. * It had not been raining heavily since morning. * My keychain had not been stolen by somebody. * The washing machine had not been used extensively.

Interrogative sentences:

Had I been going? * Had we been going? * Had you been going? * Had they been going? * Had he been going? * Had she been going? * Had it been going?

Had I been working in post office for four years? * Had we been practising golf since Monday? * Had you been working in a multinational company? * Had he been playing chess for four hours? * Had they been polishing the floor? * Had she been sitting on the chair since morning? * Had it been raining heavily since morning? * Had my keychain been stolen by somebody? * Had the washing machine been used extensively?

Interrogative negative sentences:

Had I not been going? * Had we not been going? * Had you not been going? * Had they not been going? * Had he not been going? * Had she not been going? * Had it not been going?

Had I not been working in post office for four years? * Had we not been practising golf since Monday? * Had you not been working in a multinational company? * Had he not been playing chess for four hours? * Had they not been polishing the floor? * Had she not been sitting on the chair since morning? * Had my keychain not been stolen by somebody? * Had the washing machine not been used extensively?

We have completed The PAST TENSE and its four sub-tenses and now we will write down the present, past and past participle of all verbs therein.

Regular verbs – put 'd' or 'ed' at the end perform-performed-performed, dance-danced-danced, walk-walked-walked, play-played-played, attend-attended-attended, request-requested-requested, escape-escaped-escaped, practise-practised-practised, invite-invited-invited, study-studied-studied, polish-polished-polished, use-used-used, answer-answered-answered

Irregular verbs

dig-dug-dug, drink-drank-drunk, sleep-slept-slept, read-read-read, sit-sat-sat, steal-stole-stolen

Formation of noun from verb

verb	noun	verb	noun
dance	dance	play	play
practise	practice	request	request
study	study	polish	polish
answer	answer	attend	attendance
invite	invitation		

use in sentences

Do you want to *dance*? [verb] * Find a partner and practise these *dance* steps. [noun]

There is nobody to *play* with me. [verb] * she was listening to a radio *play*. [noun]

She is *practising* that song for a week. [verb] * It is his *practice* to read several books a week. [noun]

The spelling of verb is practise and the spelling of noun is practice.

They *requested* for further assistance. [verb] * They made a *request* for further aid. [noun]

I *studied* at government medical college. [verb] * Psychology is the *study* of how human mind works. [noun]

He *polished* his shoes regularly. [verb] * I give it a *polish* now and again. [noun]

I repeated the question but she didn't *answer.* [verb] * I rang the bell but there was no *answer.* [noun]

Now we will write down the sentences in Future tense.

FUTURE TENSE

1. Simple future tense
2. Future continuous tense
3. Future perfect tense
4. Future perfect continuous tense

1. Simple future tense

Positive sentences:

I shall go. * We shall go. * You will go. * They will go. * He will go. * She will go. * It will go.

Important Note:

We can say I shall (=I will) and we shall (=we will) but not to use 'shall' with 'you', 'they', 'he', 'she', and 'it'.

I shall go to school tomorrow. * We shall go on a picnic. * You will go for a walk in the evening. * They will have their breakfast in the canteen. * He will manage to secure the admission. * She will take care of that orphan. * It will be dark in the evening.

Negative sentences:

I shall not go. * We shall not go. * You will not go. * They will not go. * He will not go. * She will not go. * It will not go.

I shall not go to school tomorrow. * We shall not go on a picnic. * You will not go for a walk in the evening. * They will not take their breakfast in the canteen. * He will not manage to secure admission. * She will not take care of that orphan. * It will not be dark in the evening.

Interrogative sentences:

Shall I go? * Shall we go? * Will they go? * Will you go? * Will he go? * Will she go? * Will it go?

Shall I go to school tomorrow? * Shall we go on a picnic? * Will you go for a walk in the evening? * Will they take their breakfast in the canteen? * Will he manage to secure admission? * Will she take care of that orphan? * Will it be dark in the evening?

Interrogative negative sentences:

Shall I not go? * Shall we not go? * Will they not go? * Will you not go? * Will he not go? * Will she not go? * Will it not go?

Shall I not go to school tomorrow? * Shall we not go on a picnic? * Will you not go for a walk in the evening? * Will they not take their breakfast in the canteen? * Will he not manage to secure admission? * Will she not take care of that orphan? * Will it not be dark in the evening?

2. Future continuous tense

Positive sentences:

I shall be going. * We shall be going. * They will be going. * You will be going. * He will be going. * She will be going. * It will be going.

I shall be going to school tomorrow. * We shall be going on a picnic. * You will be going for a walk in the evening? * They will be taking their breakfast in the canteen. * He will be managing to secure admission.

Negative sentences:

I shall not be going. * We shall not be going. * They will not be going. * You will not be going. * He will not be going. * She will not be going. * It will not be going. *

I shall not be going to school tomorrow. * We shall not be going on a picnic. * You will not be going for a walk in the evening. * They will not be taking their breakfast in the canteen. * He will not be managing to secure admission.

Interrogative sentences:

Shall I be going? * Shall we be going? * Will they be going? * Will you be going? * Will he be going? * Will she be going? * Will it be going?

Shall I be going to school tomorrow? * Shall we be going on a picnic? * Will you be going for a walk in the evening? * Will they be taking their breakfast in the canteen? * Will he be managing to secure admission?

Interrogative negative sentences:

Shall I not be going? * Shall we not be going? * Will they not be going? * Will you not be going? * Will he not be going? * Will she not be going? * Will it not be going?

Shall I not be going to school tomorrow? * Shall we not be going on a picnic? * Will you not be going for a walk in the evening? * Will they not be taking their breakfast in the canteen? * Will he not be managing to secure admission?

3. Future perfect tense

Positive sentences:

I shall have gone. * We shall have gone. * You will have gone. * They will have gone. * He will have gone. * She will have gone. * It will have gone.

I shall have completed my homework before 6 o'clock. * We shall have painted the entire building before noon. * We shall have purchased tickets before the arrival of train. * She will have knitted the sweater before her husband arrives. * They will have collected their hall tickets before the exam time. * By the next year, he will have shifted to another city.

Negative sentences:

I shall not have gone. * We shall not have gone. * You will not have gone. * They will not have gone. * He will not have gone. * She will not have gone. * It will not have gone.

I shall not have completed my homework before 6 o'clock. * We shall not have painted the entire building before noon. * We shall not have purchased the tickets before the arrival of train. * She will not have knitted the sweater before her husband arrives. * They will not have collected their hall tickets before the exam time. * By the next year, he will not have shifted to another city.

Interrogative sentences:

Shall I have gone? * Shall we have gone? * Will you have gone? * Will she have gone? * Will it have gone? * Shall I have completed my homework before 6 o'clock? * Shall we have painted the entire building before noon? * Shall we not have purchased the tickets before the arrival of train? * Will she have knitted the sweater before her husband arrives? * Will they have collected their hall tickets before the exam time? * Will he have shifted to another city, by the next year?

Interrogative negative sentences:

Shall I not have gone? * Shall we not have gone? * Will you not have gone? * Will she not have gone? * Will it not have gone?

Shall I not have completed my homework before 6 o'clock? * Shall we not have painted the entire building before noon? * Shall we not have purchased the tickets before the arrival of train? * Will she not have knitted the sweater before her husband arrives? * Will they not have collected their hall tickets before the exam time? * Will he not have shifted to another city, by the next year?

4. Future perfect continuous tense

Positive sentences:

I shall have been going. * We shall have been going. * You will have been going. * They will have been going. * He will have been going. * She will have been going. * It will have been going.

I shall have been using this chair in my old age. * We shall have been talking to him about space science. * You will have been teaching your grandson to swim. * They will have been reading for an hour before going to school. * He will have been using this car for a few years. * The patient will have been crying with pain for

a long time. * The peon will have been ringing the bell before it is seven.

Negative sentences:

I shall not have been going. * We shall not have been going. * You will not have been going. * They will not have been going. * He will not have been going. * She will not have been going. * It will not have been going.

I shall not have been using this chair in my old age. * We shall not have been talking to him about space science. * You will not have been teaching your grandson to swim. * They will not have been reading for an hour before going to school. * He will not have been using this car for a few years. * The patient will not have been crying with pain for a long time. * The peon will not have been ringing the bell before it is seven.

Interrogative sentences:

Shall I have been going? * Shall we have been going? * Will you have been going? * Will they have been going? * Will he have been going? * Will she have been going? * Will it have been going?

Shall I have been using this chair in my old age? * Shall we have been talking to him about space science? * Will you have been teaching your grandson to swim? * Will they have been reading for an hour before going to school? * Will he have been using this car for a few years? * Will the patient have been crying with a pain for a long time? * Will the peon have been ringing the bell before it is seven?

Interrogative negative sentences:

Shall I not have been going? * Shall we not have been going? * Will you not have been going? * Will they not have been going? * Will he not have been going? * Will she not have been going? * Will it not have been going?

Shall I not have been using this chair in my old age? * Shall we not have been talking to him about space science? * Will you not have been teaching your grandson to swim? * Will they not have been reading for an hour before going to school? * Will he not have been using this car for a few years? * Will the patient have not been crying with pain for a long time? * Will the peon not have been ringing the bell before seven?

Now, all the three tenses with their twelve sub-tenses are written down. We shall see the verbs therein.

Regular verbs:

manage-managed-managed, secure-secured-secured, paint-painted-painted, knit-knitted-knitted, collect-collected-collected, shift-shifted-shifted, complete-completed-completed, purchase-purchased-purchased, talk-talked-talked, cry-cried-cried

Irregular verbs:

take-took-taken, swim-swam-swum, ring-rang-rung

How did you *manage* to get it? [verb] * Who is the *manager* here? [noun]

They are *painting* the wall. [verb] * I need red *paint* for the wall. [noun]

Samples were *collected* from over 200 patients. [verb]

The total *collection* amounted to 4000 INR. [noun]

I *completed* my writing work in the morning. [verb]

The project is due for *completion* in August. [noun]

They *purchased* the land for 100000 INR. [verb]

Keep your receipt as a proof of *purchase.* [noun]

I will *ring* you up later. [verb]

He gave a couple of loud *rings* on the door bell. [noun]

Use of 'what', 'why', 'where', 'when', 'who', 'which', 'how', 'whose' and 'whom'

What do you do in the morning? * What is your name?

Why do you do like that? * Why are you angry?

Where do you go? * Where is your application?

When do you go? * When is your marriage?

Who are you? * Who is your guardian?

Which colour do you like? * Which is your book?

How are you? * How is your health?

Whose house is that? * I wonder whose this is.

(You write your own sentences for practice)

Use of 'no', 'many', 'any', 'a few', 'all', 'some', 'little', 'a little'

There is *no* water in the glass. * Just say yes or *no.*

Many people believe in God. * How *many* children do you have?

Is there *any* coffee for me? * Are there *any* stamps?

I have *a few* coins. * I need *a few* things from the store.

All trees are tall. * Cars are coming from *all* directions.

He has read *some* books. * Have *some* more vegetables.

Little water is there in the pot. [little = hardly any or no]

A little water is there in the pot. [a little = some]

(You write your own sentences for practice)

Use of 'either', 'neither', 'each', 'every'

He can take *either* side. [any of the side] * There are trees on *either* side of the road. [both sides]

Each boy had a glass of orange juice. [every one present] * We *each* have our own car. [every one]

She knows *every* student in the school. * We enjoyed *every* minute of our stay.

'Always', 'never', 'often', 'sometimes' and 'usually' go with simple present tense.

Ganesh *always* comes late to office. * *Always* lock your car. * She *always* arrives at 7.30. * she *always* criticizes me.

He *never* goes to walk alone. * You *never* help me. * He has *never* been abroad. * *Never* tell anyone your password.

I *often* see her here. * How *often* do you go to the theatre? * We *often* go there. * I have *often* wondered what happened to him.

I see him *sometimes* in this area. * He *sometimes* writes to me. * I like to be on my own *sometimes.* * *Sometimes* I go by car.

She *usually* goes to market by car. * How long does the journey *usually* take? * I am *usually* at home by 6 o'clock. * We *usually* meet here every day.

Use of 'anyone', 'someone', 'everyone', 'none', 'many', 'one'

Do you know *anyone* here? * Is *anyone* there? * Hardly *anyone* came. * Did *anyone* see you?

Someone is waiting for you. * There is *someone* at the door. * Should we call a doctor or *someone*? * *Someone* has left this bag behind.

Where is *everyone*? * *Everyone* has a chance to win. * *Everyone* cheered and clapped.* The police questioned *everyone* in the room.

None knows me in the school. [none = no one] * *None* of these pens works. * We have three sons but *none* of them lives nearby. * We saw several houses but *none* we really liked.

Many of these mangoes are raw yet. * *Many* people feel that the law should be changed. * *Many* of those present disagreed. * There are too *many* mistakes in this essay.

One should perform ones duty properly. * There is only room for *one* person. * *One* place I would really like to visit is France. * Do you want *one* or two?

Use of 'since' and 'for'

'since' is used before a point of time since morning, since last week, since last month, since 1980, since march, etc.

We have lived here *since* 2006. * I haven't eaten *since* breakfast. * She has been off work *since* Tuesday. * He has been working in a bank *since* leaving school.

'for' is used with a period of time for a long time, for ten years, for the last week, for many days, for the last month, etc.

I have been learning English *for* five years. * ~~I have been learning English since five years.~~

She has been living here *for* a long time. * I am doing this exercise *for* many days. * She has not sung *for* ten days.

Use of 'either...or', 'neither...nor'

Either the dog *or* the cat has eaten it. * *Either* the girl *or* her parents have taken it. * You may take *either* this *or* that, choice is yours. * *Either* he could not come *or* he did not want to come.

There is *neither* oxygen *nor* water on the planet Mars. * *Neither* your brother *nor* your sister seems unhappy. * *Neither* you *nor* she is to blame. * *Neither* the colour *nor* the canvas was available for painting.

Use of 'as...as', 'no sooner... than', 'not only...but also', 'so...that',

She doesn't play *as* well *as* her sister. * I haven't known him *as* long *as* you know. * He doesn't earn *as* much *as* me. * Run *as* fast *as* you can.

No sooner had he reached the railway station *than* the train arrived. * *No sooner* had she said it *than* she burst into tears.

He *not only* writes well *but also* speaks fluently. * She *not only* dances *but also* sings nicely.

The programme is *so* organized *that* none of the talks overlap. * He was *so* happy *that* he could not talk. * She worked hard *so that* everything would be ready in time.

Use of 'the'

'the' is used when it is clear which thing or person we mean.

Her office is on *the* second floor. * Turn off *the* light. * Would you like to speak to *the* manager? * Will you repeat *the* question please? * He is in *the* kitchen. * She is in *the* bathroom. * Don't forget to close *the* door. * I was cleaning *the* car. * I bought a pen and a book, *the* pen is good and *the* book is very cheap.

Use of 'hardly'

Meaning is 'almost no', 'almost not', 'almost none'

There is *hardly* any tea left. = There is no tea left. * *Hardly* anyone has bothered to reply. = Nobody has replied. * She hardly ever calls me. = She almost never calls me. * We hardly know each other. = We do not know each other. * Hardly a day goes by without my thinking of her = I think of her almost every day.

Formation of 'noun' from 'adjective'

(first word is 'adjective and second word is noun)

Only a few words are shown as ready information. For any other words, please refer to dictionary.

able – ability, absent – absence, absurd- absurdity, active – activity, agile – agility, airy – airiness, alert – alertness, adverse – adversary, acute – acuteness, adequate – adequacy, affectionate – affection, additional – addition, adorable – adoration, agile – agility, allied – alliance, answerable – answer, attractive – attraction, admirable – admiration, arrogant – arrogance, aloof – aloofness, bad – badness, bald – baldness, bloody – blood, brave – bravery, beautiful – beauty, bridal – bride, brutal – brutality, bright – brightness, barren – barrenness, biased – bias, close – closeness, capable – capability, cheap – cheapness, clean – cleanliness, clumsy – clumsiness, cold – coldness, collective – collection, colonial – colony, cool – coolness, compulsive – compulsion, cosy – cosiness, cruel – cruelty, dangerous – danger, deathly – death, doubtful – doubt, diplomatic – diplomat, dismissive – dismissal, dreamy – dream, dejected – dejection, docile – docility, duplicate – duplication, dual – duality, defective –defect, editorial – editor, elegant – elegance, emotional – emotion, estimable – esteem, equal – equality, expressive – expression, filmy – film, faithful – faithfulness, fateful – fate, fair – fairness, false – falsity, funerary – funeral, flowery – flower, familiar – familiarity, glad – gladness, green – greenery, golden – gold, gentle – gentleness, gaudy – gaudiness, hairy – hairiness, hazy – haze, holy – holiness, honourary – honour, hoarse – hoarseness, icy – iciness, ignorant – ignorance, illegible – illegibility, immune – immunity, insane – insanity, imitative – imitation, new – newness, mad – madness, nice – niceness, open – openness, oratory – orator, lenient – leniency, lawless – lawlessness, lazy – laziness, lax – laxity, mucky – muck, odd – oddness, partial – partiality, noble – nobility, noticeable – notice, obedient – obedience, opportune – opportunity, occasional – occasion, mobile – mobility, mental – mentality, mysterious – mystery, patient – patience, periodic – period, plump – plumpness, polite – politeness, portable – portability, porous – porosity, popular – popularity, private – privacy, silent – silence, secret – secrecy, satisfactory – satisfaction, shabby – shabbiness, silly – silliness, slack – slackness, saline – salinity, regular – regularity, reliable – reliability, rowdy – rowdiness, reversible – reversal, supreme – supremacy, successful – success, simple – simplicity, stale – staleness, systematic – system, tolerable – tolerance, total – totality, ugly – ugliness, tight – tightness, vague – vagueness, valid – validity, wild – wildness, visible – visibility, ultimate – ultimatum, fastidious – fastidiousness, versatile – versatility, vehement – vehemence, eccentric – eccentricity

Formation of 'noun' from 'verb'

(First word is 'verb' and second word is 'noun')

Only a few words are shown as ready information. For any other word, please refer to dictionary.

abandon – abandonment, abduct – abduction, abolish – abolition, absorb – absorption, accelerate – acceleration, accept – acceptance, accord – accordance, accuse – accusation, achieve –achievement, acquire – acquisition, activate – activation, add – addition, admire – admiration, adore – adoration, advance – advancement, advertise – advertisement, agree – agreement, allege – allegation, allocate – allocation, allot – allotment, appear – appearance, banish – banishment, calculate – calculation, cancel – cancellation, clear – clearance, collect – collection, commit – commitment, compare – comparison, compete – competition, complain – complainant, confess – confession, decimate – decimation, detect – detection, define – definition, demolish – demolition, direct – direction, discuss – discussion, discover – discovery, divide – division, educate – education, elect – election, teach – teacher, enclose – enclosure, explode – explosion, flatten – flatness, wrestle – wrestler, gather – gathering, govern – government, gyrate –gyration, help – helper, hurry – hurry, ignite – ignition, illuminate – illumination, illustrate – illustration, imagine – imagination, immerse – immersion, impress – impression, incite – incitement, indicate – indication, infer – inference, inform – information, introduce – introduction, investigate – investigation, irritate – irritation, leak – leakage, learn – learner, liberate – liberation, loiter – loiterer, lubricate – lubrication, manage – management, marry – marriage, mediate – mediator, meet – meeting, merge – merger, oblige – obligation, observe – observer, occupy – occupation, pay – payment, penalize – penalty, percolate – percolation, persuade – persuasion, possess – possession, pray – prayer, produce – production, protect – protection, quote – quotation, reduce – reduction, repeat – repetition, salute - salutation, satisfy – satisfaction, scavenge – scavenger, survey – surveyor

Formation of 'adverb' from 'adjective'

Only a few words are shown as ready information. For other words please refer to dictionary.

(first word is 'adjective' and second word is 'adverb')

abnormal – abnormality, abusive – abusively, acceptable – acceptably, active – actively, adequate – adequately, adverse – adversely, accurate – accurately, aimless – aimlessly, alphabetical – alphabetically, alternate – alternately, annual – annually, apparent – apparently, approximate – approximately, arguable – arguably, artificial – artificially, audible – audibly, attractive – attractively, automatic – automatically, avid – avidly, awkward – awkwardly, beautiful – beautifully, bitter – bitterly, blind – blindly, blissful – blissfully, bold – boldly, bossy – bossily, bright – brightly, brilliant – brilliantly, candid – candidly, capable – capably, careful – carefully, careless – carelessly, cheap – cheaply, cheerful – cheerfully, clean – cleanly, clear – clearly, close – closely, cold – coldly, dear – dearly, deep – deeply, dense – densely, distant – distantly, drastic – drastically, dutiful – dutifully, earnest – earnestly, easy – easily, elegant – elegantly, ethical – ethically, excellent – excellently, exclusive – exclusively, exotic – exotically, exquisite – exquisitely, faithful – faithfully, final – finally, firm – firmly, fitful – fitfully, flexible – flexibly, fluent – fluently, frank – frankly, grateful – gratefully, harsh – harshly, idle – idly, illicit – illicitly, initial – initially, insane – insanely, joyful – joyfully, just – justly, lame – lamely, lawful – lawfully, lazy – lazily, legal – legally, legible – legibly, light – lightly, mad – madly, meek – meekly, minimal – minimally, mindless – mindlessly, mobile

– mobility, notable – notably, obedient – obediently, original – originally, perky – perkily, permanent – permanently, plain – plainly, poor – poorly, possible – possibly, quick – quickly, quiet – quietly, rare – rarely, rash – rashly, ready – readily, reckless – recklessly, restless – restlessly, short – shortly, several – severally, shaky – shakily, smart – smartly, shy – shyly, sober – soberly, solemn – solemnly, smooth – smoothly, smug – smugly, sorrowful – sorrowfully, special – specially, specific – specifically, spotless – spotlessly, speedy – speedily, static – statically, statistical – statistically, stiff – stiffly, stony – stonily, strange – strangely, strict – strictly, strong – strongly, stunning – stunningly, stylish – stylishly, subtle – subtly, successful – successfully, suitable – suitably, supreme – supremely, surgical – surgically, sweet – sweetly, swift – swiftly, tame – tamely, tangible – tangibly, tardy – tardily, technical – technically, tender – tenderly, tentative – tentatively, thankful – thankfully, thin – thinly, thirsty – thirstily, tight – tightly, timid – timidly, tireless – tirelessly, tolerable – tolerably, torpid – torpidly, total – totally, typical – typically, unconditional – unconditionally, unfair – unfairly, unhappy – unhappily, uniform – uniformly, universal – universally, unmistakable – unmistakably, unpleasant – unpleasantly, unreasonable – unreasonably, untidy – untidily, unwilling – unwillingly, useless – uselessly, vague – vaguely, valiant – valiantly, various – variously, vehement – vehemently, verbal – verbally, vertical – vertically, vibrant – vibrantly, vicious – viciously, vigilant – vigilantly, vigour – vigourously, wary – warily, wan – wanly, visual – visually, voluble – volubly, wasteful – wastefully, virtual – virtually.

Sentences for Different Situations

Can I help you? * Do you need any help? * May be, I could help her do it. * I will help you if you like. * Let me help you. * You seem to be having some problem. * Allow me to write it for you. * Permit me to help you. * Would you like me open the windows? * Well, if you have any more problems, just let me know. * I will do it for you. * I will ring for the office boy.

Please give my regards to Suresh. * Give my best wishes to your mother. * Say hello to Rani. * Please remember me to Sumitra. * Give my sweet love to your children. * Don't forget to remember me to Anil. * Give my regards to your uncle.

That's extremely good of you. [that's = that is] * You are most kind. * I'm all right, thank you. [I'm = I am] * That's very kind of you. * I hope to get there next week. * Hopefully, she will bring it with her. * I hope to see him soon. * I hope she will do it.

It could be Amita. * May be it's that engineer. [it's = it is] * She has got a wart on her cheek. * She has a slight limp. * It's your sister on the phone. * She has a scar on her forehead. * I suppose that must be him. * There is a big mole on her chin. * I am a client of his.

Do you know who he is? * Who on earth told you that? * What colour is it? * Are you policemen? * Do you have any identification with you? * What make is his car? * See that thing there? What is it? * What time is it? * Are you on the telephone? * How much is the fare to Pune? * How much is he asking for the rent?

I don't know who it is. * There is someone at the door. * He just reminds me of someone. * I haven't the faintest idea. * I haven't a clue. * God knows, I am not sure. * I only saw his back. * But I can't put a name to his face. * I know his face but I can't place him. * I am in two minds whether to do it or not. * He is a bit uncertain about it. * I'll possibly be able to do it. [I'll = I will] * I am not sure what to do next. * I don't know whether to accept it or not.

Excuse me do you know the way to railway station? * Is there a good hotel around here? * What time is Nagpur express due in, please? * How much is the fare to Pune? * Will you please tell me how to get to this address? * When is the Ajmer express due? * Is this the right road to Goa? * You haven't got a clue, have you? * Are you on the phone?

I must go and meet him. * I simply must do it. * Do stay for dinner. * You must stay for tea. * I insist you do it. * I insist on a written report from you. * I am sorry, I can't accept that. * You really must help her. * It's essential that you meet her. * If you don't help me, I would like to see the manager. * I don't mind waiting. It is very important. * Buy the best you can afford. * Go to the counter over there. * Make out a cheque for Rs. 10000. * Take care while crossing the road. * Move to the front. * See that all the windows are closed. * Ask her to telephone me at my residence. * He should never go there again. * Keep moving, everybody. * Do not turn this box upside down. * Make out a receipt, will you? * Signal when you turn. * Don't accept anything but the best.

I will wait until you come. * I have no intension of leaving. * I'm considering leaving this place. * I plan to invite them all. * I've made up my mind to stay here for a few weeks. [I've = I have] * I'll help you and I mean it. * I am going to stay in and watch TV.

Are you busy? * How about a cup of tea? * Will you join us for a cup of tea? * What about a cup of tea? * Ah Sunil, come and join us. * How would you like to come and stay with us? * Come in and make yourself at home. Wouldn't you stay for dinner? [wouldn't = would not] * Do you feel like a cup of tea? * Can you stay for lunch?

Thank you very much. * When do you want me to come? * That would be fine. Who else is going with us? * All right. Where shall we meet then? * I am most grateful to you. * Yes, great, delighted. * I would love to attend the ceremony. * I would be glad to. Where shall we meet then? * It's very kind of you. * Sorry Ramesh, I have something else fixed up on coming Sunday. * I have already promised to attend another meeting on coming Sunday.

I must hurry otherwise I am going to be late. * Goodbye for now. * I must hurry, I am really pressed for time. * So long! Take care! * Well I must be off then. *See you again soon. * I am glad to have seen you Seema. * I must dash. * Bye, all! * Take care of yourself! * Bye, have a good time. * Thanks for coming. * It was nice to have seen you. * Have a good week end. * Come back soon. * See you later.* Must you go so soon? * Look after yourself. * I will be looking forward to see you again.

A girl with a fair complexion isn't necessarily a beautiful girl. * Big men are not necessarily strong men. * That must be Thomas. * If he is not there, he must be with Karan.

* It can't be his wife because she is here with my sister. * That can't be Susan, she is in Mumbai. * There is a lot of noise from next door. * They must be having a party or something.

He is angry with her, I think. * He is quite popular among them, I feel. * As I see it, he has no alternative but to resign. * Well, I may be wrong, but you shouldn't have said that. * If he pays you back, you must consider yourself lucky. * She was a bit careless, wasn't she? * As far as I can see, it is a gang war.

I prefer lemon juice. * I prefer my sleeves long. * I prefer swimming to cycling. * I have a preference for classical music. * I prefer that one to this, actually. * If you don't mind, I would like to have a smaller one. * I prefer staying at home. * I would rather go for a film than sit here and watch the TV.

I wish tomorrow was Monday. * I wish I were tall. * I wish I had never met him. * I wish I were rich. * I wish I knew what was going to happen. * If I had enough money, I would buy a new car. * I wish I knew what was happening. * It would be nice to have a trouble free car. * If I had enough money, I would have planned a visit to France.

Could you say that again? * Pardon? * I beg your pardon. * Could you repeat that please? * I am afraid I didn't quite get that. * What was that? * I didn't get it. * I did not quite catch what you said.

That mad person stood there in the nude. * She put the washing in the sun to dry it off. * Yellow and red colours certainly go together. * Will you thread this needle for me? * He undressed before going to bed. * He was completely naked. * Are you hanging out the washings? * Let's put the washing out; everything will be dry in half an hour. * A suit and sandals do not go together. * The boy was half naked. * She needs a size 14 dress. * Get your clothes off quickly. * She sat in front of the mirror and made up her face.

Is it raining now? * The rain poured down all day long. * How is the weather? Is it raining? * It is pouring. We can't go out. * What a pouring wet day! * It rained steadily throughout the night. * Today is a cloudless day; very bright and sunny. * The weather is fine and nice today. * The rain has wet her through.

It is drizzling. [= it is raining lightly] * The skies are clear today. * The old tree was blown down in a storm. * She took shelter from the rain under a tree. * I am drenched to the skin. [= I am totally wet.] * The dog went out and sat in a patch of sunlight. * The wind blew his cap off. * The skies remained sunny today. * It hailed last night. * My glasses are all fogged up. * A strong breeze started to blow. * It was a calm, cloudless day. * The climate there is cold. * The sky is clear; there is a cheerful atmosphere. * It is totally dark; there is no sun visible. * The sky is starry tonight. * It is a full moon day.

I am a little short of money at the moment. * She is a little short of funds at the moment. * Could you change a hundred rupees note? * How much cash have you got with you? * When he was a minister, he built up a lot of wealth. * If you pay cash, you may get some money off. * Their wages are paid weekly. * She can claim back her travelling expenses. * All her savings are in the bank. * What's the exchange rate of dollar today? * I am down to my last ten rupees. * He is a miser; he hates spending money. * I can't buy the car now; money is tight at the moment. * Ask about the price. * He comes from a rich family. * They are desperately poor.

He has no interest in music. * She took her children to a restaurant. * I love watching magic tricks. * He is showing an interest in music. * He used to do circus stunts. * He's been living a life of ease. * Let's go out and watch a film. * Have fun! * Everyone wants to live in comfort. * Don't play your radio so loud. * He doesn't like mixing business and pleasure. * You can't fish in this river. * You can't stop us fishing in the sea. * What do you do in your free time? * Play the radio a little louder, will you? * Let us go to the cinema tonight. * He is planning to throw a birthday party. * What's playing at the theatre? * He takes pleasure in eating. * I like fresh fish. * It was a fun evening. * His jokes never get many laughs. * We had a lot of fun at the party last night. * Do you like watching TV shows?

Please don't try to shout me down. * I will try my level best to help her. * Your general knowledge is as good as hers. * I took his mother as his sister. * Have you hung out the washings? * Mind your head, the door frame is low. * She is as busy as a bee. * The man is as timid as a rabbit. * The little girl's cheeks are as red as a rose. * Delhi to Kanpur is 300 kilometres as the crow flies. * When I reached Mumbai, it was raining cats and dogs. * Although Jagdish had worked hard, he failed in the exam. * As long as I am here, you need not worry about anything. * I am not as bad as you think. * I know neither you nor your sister. * Either you or your brother gave me this book. * My watch is not going. * He has a lot of go in him. [= lot of courage in him] * Let us have another go at the problem. [= try one more time] * He is a go-getter. [go-getter = adventurous] * His story holds water. [= his statement is true] * Radha is not in speaking terms with Ramesh. * Happiness doesn't always go with riches. * She has a sweet tooth. [= She likes sweet eatables.] * Are you out of your head? * Are you out of your mind? * Please do not jump the queue. [= Please come in the queue.] * The cat nosed out the rat. [= The cat smelled the rat.]

Our neighbor kicked the bucket at the age of 90. [to kick the bucket = to die] * Do not poke your nose in my affairs. * She is a purse proud lady. [purse proud = proud of richness] * I am taller than you. * My wife is more talkative than yours. * Now the condition of patient is much better than that of yesterday. * The shirt is too short in sleeves. * It's time to go to bed. * It's time to retire. [= It's time to go to bed.] * It is at the tip of my tongue. * He wore the shirt inside out. * After lunch, I was having forty winks. [to have forty winks = to take a short sleep] * It was a windless day. * The dog is limping.

That man, who is he? = Who is that man? * Our new boss, have you met him? = Have you met our new boss? * That boy, I have seen somewhere. = I have seen that boy somewhere. * Your friend, what is his name? = What is the name of your friend? * My wife, she is from Calcutta. = Meet my wife, she is from Calcutta.

Topic Changers

'fine', 'by the way', 'anyhow', 'all right', 'okay', 'good', etc are the topic changers. These are used to change topic while speaking.

example:

Have you said everything you want to? *Fine*, let us move on to next subject.

The sweets you gave are delicious; *by the way*, I am going to Delhi tomorrow.

The train doesn't leave until ten; *anyhow*, what do you think of my new dress?

Send the reply today evening; *all right*, where is the money I gave you?

Have you finished it? *Good*, take rest now.

I have a headache; *anyway*, what is your problem?

I have gone through the papers; *anyway*, let us see the guest now.

It is your private matter; *by the way*, what about the export order?

She has brought the kids to office; *by the way*, why are you so late today?

Have you finished your typing? *Fine,* let me see the cxport file.

It is you who told me that she is married; *anyhow*, where is my consignment?

Has she come to office? *Fine*, bring my red file.

Sentences Using

will, would, shall, should, can, could, may, might, must, ought, dare, need, used to

He *will* study for the exam. * During the summer flowers *will* fade. * They *will* speak about the girls only. * They *will* always walk on the footpath. * She *will* never remain silent. * She *will* take you to her home. * You *will* visit him as usual. * They *will* leave as soon as the rain stops. * Farmers *will* cultivate the land before sowing.

Would you mind reading this letter for her? * *Would* you please speak in English? * *Would* you please move ahead? * I *would* like to come with you. * They *would* like to stay here tonight. * *Would* you mind if I take this book? * *Would* you please convey my message to them?

I *shall* meet her next Sunday. * We *shall* give him a gift. * I *shall* not talk to you again. * We *shall* have a dinner party tonight. * We *shall* be warned for our misconduct. * *Shall* I wait for her? * *Shall* we go to the library? * *Shall* we start the function?

Note: 'shall' is used only for 'I' and 'we', and not for 'you', 'he', 'she', 'it' and 'they'

Students *should* obey their elders. * People *should* not throw waste on the road. * Teachers *should* advise the pupils to study hard. * Parents *should* take care of their children. * Soldiers *should* maintain discipline to win the war. * People *should* behave decently during the public functions.

He *can* swim well. * She *can* dance well. * You *can* take rest, if you need. * She *can* sing well. * I *can* walk to railway station. * They *can* go to sleep, if they feel like. * We *can* easily cross the bridge. * We *can* see the traffic from our gallery.

I *could* play tennis when I was young. * He *could* swim well in his youth. * We *could* play cricket when we were young. * *Could* I have a glass of juice? * *Could* I go with him to see the exhibition? * You *could* have finished earlier.

May I come in sir? * You *may* eat that fruit. * *May* I take your bicycle? * He *may* be at home. * She *may* come to see me. * *May* I have your book? * *May* we go to market? * *May* I sit here? * *May* I accompany you to city? * *May* be, he is coming late.

I *might* go home tomorrow. * My father *might* not allow me to go on tour. * I *might* have achieved it. * She *might* not go to market. * They *might* be right. * They *might* not know that the doctor is here.

Children must respect their elders. * Everybody *must* take physical exercises. * She *must* be very clever. * *Must* she do it for herself? * *Must* he go to college today? * *Must* we not stand up when the teacher arrives? * *Must* he attend the course on interior decoration?

You *ought* to respect the elders. * You *ought* to study hard. * She *ought* to pass in the examination. * She *ought* to have told me the fact. * I *ought* to have been strict with him. * He *ought* to have discussed the matter with her. * She *ought* to have taken my permission.

Did he *dare* to comment on your work? * *Dare* I talk to him about her? * She *dared* to talk to her uncle. * How *dare* you talk to me? * How *dare* you disregard the rules? * How *dare* you laugh at him? * *Dare* you talk to me like that? * How *dare* you go without my consent? * Did he *dare* to attempt it? * *Dare* you do it without his consent?

I *need* not have joined him for the tuition. * You *need* not have lent him the money. * We *need* to have warned him well before. * Boys *need* to leave the classroom. * You *need* to have asked for his guidance. * You *need* to take his permission. * He *needs* to show the pass for entry.

My friend *used to* drink before his marriage. * She *used to* live with her aunt before her marriage. * I *used to* ask questions daily. * They *used to* get up early in the morning. * I *used to* go for morning walk during summer. * He *used to* drink milk every day. * I know, you *used to* visit the library regularly.

Sentences Beginning With 'Adverbs'

Cleverly she avoided all those difficulties. * *Quite likely* she was trying to avoid him. * *Confidentially* they are not satisfied with her work. * *Essentially* you should have a clear idea of the procedure. * *Evidently* he is not interested. * *Obviously* she had a nice time. *

Definitely she deserves some reward. * *Officially* the news hasn't been confirmed. * *Frankly* I didn't like it. * *Plainly* they don't want to give you a warm welcome. * *Privately* I didn't approve it. * *Foolishly* we decided to change the plan. * *Personally* I like it very much. * *Perhaps* this is the best time to sort out the dispute. * *Fundamentally* our legal system is very strong. * *Probably* her feet were wet. * *Possibly* many of the passengers are hurt. * *Oddly enough* the bag was empty. * *Honestly* the music affected me deeply. * *Really* you should consider yourself lucky. * *Ideally* we should consider their opinion. * *Very likely* he was afraid to tell him about it. * *Thankfully* it didn't rain on that day. * *Mercifully* it was not a serious accident. * *Rightly* they decided to call off the strike. * *Fortunately* I am on good terms with them. * *Strangely enough* they haven't even sent a reply yet. * *Most likely* he will be back in an hour. * *Most unexpectedly* certain problems cropped up. * *Funnily enough* I ran into that again in the street. * *Naturally* they couldn't believe what they heard. * *Seriously* this job needs a lot of skill and knowledge. * *Luckily* you got the train to Delhi. * *Clearly* it is the case of sheer negligence.

Use of 'to', 'ing', 'or', 'but', 'and', 'if', etc.

Sentences beginning with 'to'

To be fair, he must get all the credit.

To be frank, I don't think this dress suits you at all.

To be honest, we don't have enough money for all this.

To judge from what he said, he seems to be an expert in this subject.

To be precise, this happened on 15th of July last year.

To put it frankly, I never expect him to behave like that.

-ing sentences

Frankly *speaking*, I don't like people playing jokes on others. * Generally *speaking*, jobs like these take long time to complete. * *Putting* it bluntly, you take it too seriously. * *Putting* it crudely, they don't care two hoots about all this. * *Putting* it frankly, we don't want to charge them for damage. * *Putting* it mildly, your criticism was a bit too much. * Roughly *speaking*, he draws about 70000 Rupees a month. * *Speaking* frankly, neither of them is correct. * Strictly *speaking*, he is a captain and not a major general. * *Speaking* personally, I feel some hesitation. * *Speaking* purely for myself, I liked that film very much.

attention drawing sentences

Mr. Sharma, please look at me. * Excuse me, are these yours? * Mary, give it to me. * Madam, please come here. * Listen to me kids. * Sir, can I have a word with you? * What's for dinner mom? * You fool, that is not the way to do it. * Don't do that darling. * That's all, ladies and gentlemen. * Doctor, is it anything serious?

sentences beginning with compliment

Sweet, those flowers smelt. * *Very calm*, she was. * *Very strange*, her voice sounded. * *Above five feet tall*, she was. * *Very heavy*, that box felt. * *Guilty*, the judge found him. * *Rather bitter*, the tea tasted. * *Very odd*, everybody found what happened. * *An expert*, he has become. * *A good idea*, it sounded. * *Chairman*, they elected him. * *Clean and tidy*, you should keep your room. * *Very serious*, the whole situation was.

sentences using 'or'

We can go to the film *or* we can go to the museum. * He must have killed her *or* he knows who killed her. * You can call him back *or* you can leave a message. * He doesn't like this job *or* that's what he said. * That must be an old car *or* that's not in good condition. * You must be very careful *or* you will make mistakes. * You write it down *or* get a Xerox copy of it.

sentences using 'but'

She saw him *but* she didn't smile at him. * He panicked *but* she remained calm. * Our income hasn't increased *but* our expenses have gone up considerably. * I am all for this campaign *but* I am not happy with the way it is planned. * I will wait for you *but* you should hurry up. * I will explain it to them *but* I am doubtful whether they will understand me correctly. * She was ready to give a lecture *but* there were no students. * I am ready to accompany you *but* not on coming Sunday.

sentences using 'and'

He saw the smoke *and* he raised the alarm. * She did well in the interview *and* she got the job. * Sales have improved *and* there will be profit this year. * Life is splendid and we are quite happy here. * He opened the door and flicked the light switch on. * He is a bit reserved and she is very outgoing. * He works hard and yet they are not satisfied. * Give him some money and he will do it for you.

sentences using 'if' [conditional sentences]

The sentences wherein 'if' is used are conditional sentences.

If you heat the butter, it melts.

If you don't work, you will not pass.

If he walks faster, he will catch the bus.

If she had told me, I would have helped her.

The above sentences may be written in reverse order without any change in meaning.

example:

Butter melts *if* you heat it.

You will not pass *if* you don't work hard.

He will catch the bus *if* he walks faster.

I would have helped her *if* she had told me.

Note: The comma will not be there when 'if' is in the middle of sentences.

If I go shopping, I will buy some fruits.

If it rains, we won't play the match.

If you overeat, you will be fat.

Observe the above sentences written in reverse order without any change in meaning.

I will buy some fruits *if* I go shopping.

We won't play the match *if* it rains.

You will be fat *if* you overeat.

You may use 'unless' and 'supposing that' in place of 'if'.

example:

Unless you work harder, you will not succeed. = *If* you don't work harder, you will not succeed. = You will not succeed *if* you don't work harder.

Unless we hurry, we shall miss the train. = *If* we do not hurry, we shall miss the train. = We shall miss the train *if* we do not hurry.

Supposing that it rains, can we hold the meeting in the hall? = *If* it rains, can we hold the meeting in the hall? = Can we hold the meeting in the hall *if* it rains?

Exclamatory sentences

What – exclamations:

What a beautiful day! * What a beautiful smile your sister has! * What a day! * What a clever student she is! * What a dull book! * What a lovely house! * What a horrid cup of tea! * What a funny thing to say! * What a nuisance she is! * What a mess! * What a horrible song! * What a miserable day!

How exclamations:

How awkward! * How cleverly you hid your feelings! * How splendidly they played! * How generous they have been! * How nice of you to come! * How nice you look! * How dare you speak to me like that! * How I used to like it! * How lucky you are! * How cute! * How beautifully you sing!

Miscellaneous exclamations:

A chance of a lifetime! * Breakfast in bed! * Do up your buttons! * Bad luck! * Better luck next time! * Good lord! * Good heavens! * He is no chicken! * Many happy returns of the day! * My goodness! * Most kind of you! * Oh God! * Quite a show! * Stuff and nonsense! * Stupendous! * Wonderful news! * Well done! * Take look in the mirror! * Very nice of you! * Very kind of you!

Negative exclamatory sentences:

Aren't you lucky! * Isn't he a fool! * Wouldn't you believe! * Isn't she clever! * Isn't that strange! * Isn't the weather nice! * Isn't he like his father! * Isn't she smart! * Wasn't it a splendid show! * Aren't these mangoes sweet!

Positive exclamatory sentences:

Have you heard anything like it! * Am I crazy! * Am I tired! * Was she thrilled! * Am I glad to be home! * Did she look surprised! * I am so thankful to you! * Can I ever thank you enough!

One word exclamations:

Cheers! * Colossal! * Delightful! * Excellent! * Fantastic! * Fine! * Good! * Great! * Magnificent! * Marvellous! * Ridiculous! * Rubbish! * Rot! * What! * Unbelievable

To – exclamations

To think that he could be so cruel! * To think that I might have been killed! * To think that she was a spy! * To think she would leave him! * To think that he would deny our request! * To think that things would come to this stage!

Sentences – Correct / Incorrect

Correct	Incorrect
I didn't know.	I didn't knew.
He didn't like it.	He didn't liked it.
She didn't speak French.	She didn't spoke French.
It didn't happen often.	It didn't happened often.
We didn't buy things.	We didn't bought things.
They didn't worry.	They didn't worried.
The car didn't start.	The car didn't started.
I don't know.	I don't knew.
He doesn't like it.	He doesn't liked it.
I had done it.	I had did it.
He had stolen it.	He had stole it.
She had written it down.	She has wrote it down.
She had hidden it.	She had hid it.
We hadn't eaten it.	We hadn't ate it.
They have not spoken.	They have not spoke.
They had taken it away.	They had took it away.
The show hadn't begun.	The show hadn't began

Negative meaning sentences:

They seldom come to agreement. = They never come to agreement. * It is worth hardly anything. = It is worthless. * He said nothing to them. = He didn't say anything to them. * She was barely able to talk. = She was unable to talk. * I could scarcely believe my eyes. = I could not believe what I saw. * I never had a desire for it. = I did not desire it at all. * Not everybody can go inside. = Only a few can go inside.

Degrees of Comparison

1. Positive degree:

example - Karan is smart. * She is beautiful

2. Comparative degree:

example - Karan is smarter than others.

She is more beautiful than others.

3. Superlative degree:

example - Karan is the smartest in the class.

She is the most beautiful girl

Formation of comparative and superlative degrees:

Positive	comparative	Superlative
bold	bolder	boldest
clever	cleverer	cleverest
great	greater	greatest
sweet	sweeter	sweetest
easy	easier	easiest
happy	happier	happiest
heavy	heavier	heaviest
merry	merrier	merriest
wealthy	wealthier	wealthiest
able	abler	ablest

brave	braver	bravest
fine	finer	finest
wise	wiser	wisest
sad	sadder	saddest
white	whiter	whitest
large	larger	largest
noble	nobler	noblest
big	bigger	biggest
thin	thinner	thinnest
fat	fatter	fattest
Positive	**Comparative**	**Superlative**
hot	hotter	hottest
red	redder	reddest
good	better	best
bad	worse	worst
many	more	most
much	more	most
little	less	least
old	older	oldest
late	later	latest
beautiful	more beautiful	most beautiful
less beautiful	least beautiful	
qualified	more qualified	most qualified
less qualified	least qualified	
cautious	more cautious	most cautious

less cautious	least cautious	
kind	more kind	most kind
less kind	least kind	
proper	more proper	most proper
less proper	least proper	
ordinary	more ordinary	most ordinary
less ordinary	least ordinary	

Interchange of the degree of comparison:

He is the cleverest boy in the class.

He is cleverer than any other boy in the class.

He is the cleverest boy in the class.

He is cleverer than most other boys in the class.

Study the following examples;

Delhi is a big city.	= positive
Delhi is bigger than other cities.	= comparative
Delhi is the biggest city.	= superlative
Kalidas was a great poet.	= positive
Kalidas was greater than other poets.	= comparative
Kalidas was the greatest of all poets.	= superlative
Darasingh was a strong man.	= positive
Darasingh was stronger than others.	= comparative
Darasingh was the strongest of men.	= superlative
It was a good story.	= positive
It was better than other stories.	= comparative
It was the best of all stories.	= superlative

He is intelligent. = positive

He is more intelligent than others. = comparative

He is the most intelligent. = superlative

She is a smart girl. = positive

She is smarter than others. = comparative

She is the smartest of all girls. = superlative

I am a tall boy. = positive

I am a taller boy than others. = comparative

I am the tallest of all the boys. = superlative

You are a wise girl. = positive

You are wiser than other girls. = comparative

You are the wisest of all girls. = superlative

Lion is a strong animal. = positive

Lion is stronger than other animals. = comparative

Lion is the strongest of all animals. = superlative

Active and Passive voice:

Present simple tense

We make butter from milk. - active voice

Butter is made from milk. - passive voice

Somebody cleans this room. - active voice

This room is cleaned by somebody. - passive voice

People never invite her to parties. - active voice

She is never invited to parties. - passive voice

How do they make butter? - active voice

How is butter made? - passive voice

Past simple tense

Somebody stole my car last week. - active voice

My car was stolen last week. - passive voice

When did they build these houses? - active voice

When were these houses built? - passive voice

They didn't invite me to the party. - active voice

I was not invited to the party. - passive voice

Somebody stole my keys yesterday. - active voice

My keys were stolen yesterday. - passive voice

Present continuous tense

They are building a new airport. - active voice

A new airport is being built by them. - passive voice

They are building new houses. - active voice

New houses are being built by them. - passive voice

Past continuous tense

When I was here a few years ago, they were building a new airport. - active voice

When I was here a few years ago, a new airport was being built. - passive voice

Present perfect tense

Look! They have painted the door. - active voice

Look! The door has been painted. - passive voice

Somebody has washed them. - active voice

They have been washed. - passive voice

Past perfect tense

Amita said that somebody has stolen her car. - active voice

Amita said that her car had been stolen. - passive voice

Use of: will, must, can, have, may, should, etc.

Somebody will clean the office today. - active

The office will be cleaned today. - passive

Somebody must clean the office. - active

The office must be cleaned. - passive

He may drive the car through the tunnel. - active

The car may be driven through the tunnel. - passive

Somebody has to wash these clothes. - active

These clothes have to be washed. - passive

He can win the prize. - active

The prize can be won. - passive

Do it at once. - active

Let it be done at once. - passive

Never tell a lie. - active

Let a lie never be told. - passive

Please help the poor. - active

You are requested to help the poor. - passive

Do not gamble. - active

You are advised not to gamble. - passive

Stand up on the bench. - active

You are ordered to stand up on the bench. - passive

Questions – How To Make?

You have to be really good at asking questions in English. If you are not, do you think you will be able to have satisfactory discussion with someone?

Suppose you are at a social party in the evening or you are travelling on a train. What will make conversation to go on? It's mainly your ability to ask questions. If you are not able to ask questions, you will find it difficult to continue the conversation and it will come to a stop. You will be a silent listener. People around will go away with a wrong impression about you – that you do not know English. If you want to carry on discussion in any field, you have to be good at asking questions in fluent English. Suppose you want some information from someone, what alone will help you get the information? It is your skill in putting questions. If you ask someone about something, he will give you some reply. If you are not satisfied with the reply, you have to ask another question. You will get a reply. If you are fully satisfied, you will not have any more questions. It means you have to go on asking more questions, right kind of questions.

Difficulty in framing questions:

Many educated people are able to produce questions correctly in writing. But when they have to produce a question in speech, they falter and fail. Many times, they produce the questions wrongly as shown below. These are a few examples.

Right	**Wrong**
What are you doing?	What you are doing?
Where have you put it?	Where you have put it?
When did you come?	When you came?

Right	**Wrong**
How are you?	How you are?
Will you do it?	Whether you will do it?
Can he come?	Whether he can come?
Is he coming?	Whether he is coming?
How is she managing?	How she is managing?

At other times, they end up muttering nonsense. They become nervous and keep silent. Finally, they switch on to their mother tongue.

Therefore it is time for us to pay close attention to question patterns. You should know that making questions is one of the most essential skill in spoken English. We have to master that skill. Don't worry! It can be mastered by regular practice.

You will never be able to learn 'right' question patterns from the list of 'right' and 'wrong' samples. You have to get the 'right' question pattern imprinted on your mind so that it will not fade away. They will remain in your mind and help you to make the 'right' question at the right spot.

Ashok is a good boy. This is a statement.

Is Ashok a good boy? This is a question.

Here, note the reversal of the arrangement of verb and subject.

If you want to speak English fluently, the right order of words must come easily. It may be a statement, it may be a question or it may be an exclamation. The right order of words must come in your mind easily without any loss of time.

Here, I would like to stress that the *loud reading* and *repetition* is necessary for gaining fluency in spoken English.

Read aloud the following questions as many times as possible. It will help you to make questions of different types in different situations.

Question Types

'Yes-No' questions (positive)

'Yes-No' questions are questions that expect 'yes' or 'no' as a reply. The most common word for confirmation is 'yes' and most common word for negation is 'no'. Following are the few examples of 'yes-no' questions.

Is he a nice person? * Is she coming to the wedding? * Are there any objections? * Are you ready? * Does she like coffee? * Did you paint it yourself? * Would you like an orange? * Can I come to you? * Has she been here often? * Can we do something about it? * Am I late? * Am I right? * Are you sure? * Are you still there? * Are you sure of the spelling? * Are you talking to me? * Are you there Leela? * Aren't they rather expensive? * Aren't you doing anything? * Is your birthday on fourth? * Isn't she very bright? * Isn't that special? * Were you talking to me? * Were you waiting for a long time?

Do you really think that it is wrong? * Do you understand what I am saying? * Do the others like it? * Do you have anything smaller? * Do you like it? * Does the journey take that long? * Does this drug have any side effects? * Did you hear any strange noise? * Did you say you couldn't play? * Did you meet Ramesh? * Do you wish to play? * Did she go to temple? * Does the flag have four colours? *

Have you seen a doctor? * Have you seen my gold watch? * Have you seen my pen? * Have you been introduced?

* Have you bought the car? * Has he left already? * Has the meeting started? * Has she met you yesterday? * Has it been raining? * Has she spoken to him? * Have you any money to buy a book?

Can you see that? * Can you drive? * Can you get this stain out? * Can you gift-wrap that? * Could you please repeat that? * Could you speak louder? * Could you please speak lower? * Could you please move aside a little?

May I see some identification? * May I see the wine list? * May I see your boarding pass? * May I take your leave? * May I come in? * May I sit here? * May I take your pen? * May I come with you?

Must you leave so soon? * Must he sleep in the tent? * Must I do this work? * Must they go now? * Must you write the letter? * Must she go to market? * Must I give it to you?

Shall we go for a walk daddy? * Shall we go for swimming? * Shall we go today? * Shall we have a game of chess? * Shall we go to a movie? * Shall we go for a long drive? * Shall we go for hunting?

Will you hold it for me? * Will you join us? * Will you lend a hand Smita? [= Will you help me, Smita?] * Will you lend me your pen? * Would you like to schedule your next appointment? * Would you like to see the menu card? * Would you like to sit over here? * Would you like to have a cup of tea?

Make questions from statements:

He is leaving tomorrow. – Is he leaving tomorrow?

He can start his work. – Can he start his work?

You will forget it. – Will you forget it?

He has been waiting. – Has he been waiting?

He is able to read English. – Is he able to read English?

He looks nice. – Does he look nice?

They work here. – Do they work here?

She cried a lot. – Did she cry a lot?

He knows the answer. – Does he know the answer?

She loves cartoons. – Does she love cartoons?

They hate him. – Do they hate him?

I am wrong. – Am I wrong?

He is an engineer. – Is he an engineer?

She is his sister. – Is she his sister?

He is very tall. – Is he very tall?

They are very excited. – Are they very excited?

She is in the kitchen. – Is she in the kitchen?

He is on a diet? – Is he on a diet?

He does his job well. – Does he do his job well?

He has a new car. – Does he have a new car?

She has a long hair. – Does she have a long hair?

He has a headache. – Does he have a headache?

We have no option. – Do you have any option?

She has got a car. – Has she got a car?

She has got a long hair. – Has she got a long hair?

We have got no option. – Have we got any option?

He hasn't got any change. – Hasn't he got any change?

They haven't got any regrets at all.	– Haven't they got any regrets at all?
They haven't got any time to wait.	– Haven't they got any time to wait?
He has lunch at 12 noon every day.	– Does he have lunch at 12 noon every day?
They have a swim in the sea.	– Do they have a swim in the sea?
They have tea together in the evening.	– Do they have tea together in the evening?
He had an operation last week.	– Did he have an operation last week?
They had a quarrel yesterday.	– Did they have a quarrel yesterday?
She didn't have breakfast today.	– Didn't she have breakfast today?
Her father does the accounts for them.	– Does her father do the accounts for them?

Responses to 'yes-no' questions:

Question	**Answer**
Can I use your bathroom?	All right / OK.
Can I ask them to come in?	By all means!
Can I read your newspaper?	Certainly!
Are you telling the truth?	Honest to God.
Is that true?	Of course!
Is it safe?	Sure.
Are you happy?	Very much!
Did they blame you?	Absolutely not.

Can I show you another model?	Forget it.
Do you need their help?	Certainly not.
Is he going to come?	I think not.
Have you ever seen him angry?	Never.
Do you mind if I have a look?	Not at all!
Can I borrow your car?	Nothing doing.
Do you think he will support you?	Out of question.
Question	**Answer**
Do you think he will marry her?	Over my dead body.
[over my dead body = impossible]	
Can I have a look at it?	If you like,
Is this as good as his last book?	Better, actually.
Did you enjoy yourself?	Tremendously
Is she as beautiful as her mother?	More beautiful
Was she really so rude?	Unbelievably
Do you watch television often?	Hardly ever
Is he happy there?	May be
Is he satisfied with your work?	It appears so.
Did you like it?	Not very much
Do you eat out often?	Occasionally
Is he aware of all this?	Probably not
Is that true?	To some extent
Is she often late?	Very often
Do you mind if I smoke?	Certainly!

'Yes-No' questions (negative)

Am I not right? * Isn't he waiting for a taxi? * Isn't he his boss? * Aren't you expecting him? * Aren't they sorry? * Wasn't he a merchant? * Weren't they against the project? * Haven't they answered yet? * Doesn't he like detective books? * Didn't you find all this a bit different? * Wouldn't you like to join us for a party?

Sometimes, you can make a negative 'yes-no' question by using the negative words as follows.

in no way, neither of, never, no, no longer, no more, no one, none of, nobody, nothing, nowhere

Are you *in no way* concerned with what is going on? * Is *neither of* them interested in the offer? * Have you *never* heard of these things? * Are there *no* sales assistants here? * Do they *no longer* live here? * Are you *no more* interested in this offer? * Has *no one* got back from there? * I know *none* of them. * Did nobody complain about it? * Does *nothing* affect that man? * Is there *nowhere* for me to park the car? * There was *nowhere* for me to sit.

Everyday 'yes-no' questions for practice:

Read each question several times aloud. This is just to train your tongue. The loud reading will help to frame such questions. The more you read loudly, the better it is for fluent speaking.

be-questions

Am I going south? * Am I making myself clear? * Anything else I can do for her? * Are ladies allowed? * Are washing machines available? * Are my photos developed yet? * Are pets allowed? * Are the kids ready? * Are there any nails in the box? * Are these sets still available? * Are these tickets available extra? * Are they any good? * Are they going to be OK? * Are things getting you down? * Are cameras permitted? * Are we almost there? * Are we ready to leave?

Is the gratuity included? * Is a meal served? * Is a paper required for this course? * Are washer and drier available? * Is anyone sitting here? * Is attendance necessary for this course? * Is everything all right? * Is everything fine? * Is he angry with me?

* Is he breathing? * Is he getting fatter? * Is he tall and dark? * Is it a big house? * Is it cancer? * Is it closing time already? * Is it curable? * Is it difficult?

Was he very late? * Was it a good time? * Was it a good show? * Was it expensive? * Was it twins or triplets? * Was it well acted? * Was the play good? * Was it easy crossing the road?

do-questions

Do you agree with her? * Do you agree, John? * Do you and Mala like ice cream? * Do you both play basket ball? * Do you change your book every week? * Do you come here often? * Do you ever go to club? * Do you ever go to the theatre? * Do you follow me? * Do you have his phone number? * Do you have proof of insurance? * Do you have reservations? * Do you have senior citizen discounts? * Do you have something a bit less expensive? * Do you have something specific in your mind? * Do you have the correct time? * Do you have it in a larger size? * Do you have this in blue? * Do you have this in stock? * Do you have this in wool? * Do you have time for coffee? * Do you have to be there? * Do you have to drive this fast? * Do you have vegetarian dishes? * Do you have your bank ID card? * Do you have your keys? * Do you have your receipt? * Do you have your VISA? * Do you hear me? * Do you hear what I am saying? * Do you know French? * Do you know how much this was? * Do you know if it is a boy or a girl? * Do you know what I am talking about? * Do you know what size you are? * Do you know what the problem is? * Do you know what you want?

Do you accept cheques? * Do you get the picture? * Do you accept credit cards? * Do you agree? * Do you bake birthday cakes to order? * Do you care if I join you? * Do you carry the newspaper? * Do you come here often? * Do you do alterations on men's clothing?

Do I have to change buses? * Do I have to change planes? * Do I have to change trains? * Do I have to feed them? * Do I have to stay over Saturday night? * Do I have to stay overnight?

Does a bus go there? * Does a train go there? * Does anyone know central bus station? * Does Amit really need it? * Does he ever lend a hand? = Does he ever offer help? * Does he know? * Does he do the physical exercises?

Doesn't anyone want to do the crossword? * Don't I know you from somewhere? * Don't you get a bit lonely? * Don't you go by underground passage? * Don't you have a light in your garage? * Don't you have anything better to do?

Did any of the parents turn up? * Did he talk to you? * Did everything go OK? * Did I say you could touch that? * Did Sunita like it? * Did Meera post that letter? * Did the children behave? * Did the job take long? * Did we forget anything? * Did you bring me anything? * Did you call at the bank? * Did you call him a liar? * Did you call him? * Did you catch the last train?

have-questions

Has he been sleeping well? * Has Leela arrived yet? * Has she told them? * Has this been a problem before? * Hasn't this coupon expired? * Have Mahesh and Ramesh arrived? * Have I made myself clear? * Have I met him before? * Have they figured out what is wrong? * Have we forgotten anything? * Have you any

cigarettes left? * Have you any doubt about it? * Have you any objection? * Have you any sealing wax? * Have you been keeping busy? * Have you been driving since a long time?

can-questions

Can anyone lend me a copy? * Can Prakash borrow your penknife? * Can he play the flute? * Can he apply for a credit card? * Can I ask you a question? * Can I borrow it? * Can I borrow some bed sheets? * Can I borrow your stapler? * Can I bring my kids? * Can I bring pets? * Can I bring something? * Can I bring two guests? * Can I send the money order from here? * Can I buy you a drink? * Can I change my flight schedule? * Can I change my itinerary? [itinerary = a planned route of journey] * Can I check the oil level? * Can I check your tyres? * Can I come again on Monday? * Can I come home by myself mummy? * Can I get you something to drink? * Can I go standby? [standby = a person or a thing ready to be used in emergency]

Could I bother you for something? * Could I buy you a drink? * Could I come over later today? * Could I give you a lift? * Could I have a soda? * Could I have a word with you? * Could I have more coffee please? * Could I have some more butter? * Could I have some more water please? * Could I have someone call you? * Could I have the bill? * Could you please wait for me? * Could she not wait for you? * Could she not take it for a while? * Could I get you a glass of juice?

Could you not attend the lecture? * Could they have attended the ceremony?

may-questions

May I ask why you wish to cancel? * May I be excused? * May I be frank? * May I borrow this for a day? * May I borrow this book for a while? * May I borrow your pen? * May I bring a friend? * May I attend to your lecture? * May I come too? * May I get it gift wrapped? * May I see your receipt please? * May I have another bun? * May I come in please? * May I take your leave? * May I take a chair? = May I sit?

shall-questions

Shall I buy you a replacement? * Shall I check your oil? * Shall I come in by the front door? * Shall I get rid of it? * Shall I get you some more? * Shall I go back for it now? * Shall I go or shan't I? = Shall I go or shall I not go? * Shall I go to the meeting? * Shall I lend him mine?

Should I bring anything? * Should I call a doctor? * Should I call for the nurse? * Should I send them directly to railway station?

will-question

Will I be able to walk again? * Will he be all right? * Will he buy another one? * Will he come back? * Will it be on the sale soon? * Will it help, do you think? * Will my insurance cover this? * Will someone be joining you? * Will that be a large soft drink? * Will that be all?

Won't you be cold if you don't come inside? * Won't you come for a walk? * Won't you have some grapes? * Won't he get irritated?

Would a glass of water help? * Would anyone like coffee? * Would he subscribe, do you suppose? * Would he lend me his dictionary? * Would I lie to you? * Would I lie? * Would I like it, do you think? * Would it be a problem if I dropped by for a few minutes? * Would it be better if I left on Thursday instead? * Would it be possible to deliver this to hospital today? * Would Raju take it, do you think? * Would Prakash have a game? * Would you please gift-wrap that? * Would you accept a cigar? * Would you care for dessert? * Would you care for some nuts? * Would you care for some tea? * Would you care for some butter? * Would you make a reservation for another night? * Would you care to see the wine list? * Would you care to stay for dinner? * Would you check my tyres? * Would you check the battery? * Would you check the oil? * Would you check the shock absorbers? * Would you excuse me? * Would you give me the PIN code of Mumbai? * Would you have a look under the hood? * Would you keep or sell it? * Would you like a baked potato or rice? * Would you like a bite? * Would you like a black one or blue one?

wh-questions [positive]

Wh-questions are the questions starting with one of the following eight 'wh' words. These are not 'yes-no' questions. The reply will be explanative.

'what', 'when', 'where', 'which', 'who', 'whose', 'why', and 'how'

What is your name? * *What* will she get? * *What* do they want? * *What* did she paint? * *What* were they talking about? * *What* is he interested in? * *What* was

that noise? * *What* will the test cover? * *What* will they think of me? * *What* would you advise?

When did she see him? * *When* will Rita be back? * When is the concert? * When is their bed time? * When will you ask him then? * When is your birthday? * When do you go to market? * When are you going to play? * When is your marriage ceremony? * When is your exam? * When do you think of visiting her?

Where has she gone? * *Where* does he come from? * *Where* shall we keep it? * *Where* would you like to go? * *Where* is he? * *Where* did you go yesterday? * *Where* do you live? * *Where* did you read it? * *Where* is your school?

Which of these two do you like? * *Which* would you choose if you were me? * *Which* will you take, Harry? * *Which* one would he select? * *Which* colour is attractive? * *Which* of the applicants has got the job? * *Which* is better exercise, swimming or tennis? * *Which* way is the wind blowing?

Who opened the door? * *Who* can do it? * *Who* is next? * *Who* is on the line? * *Who* has got it then? * *Who* is that woman? * *Who* are you? * *Who* is she? * *Who* are they? * *Who* is there? * *Who* is staying in that room? * *Who* is it?

Whose house is that? * *Whose* purse is this? * *Whose* is the new bike? * *Whose* book is that? * *Whose* is this compass box? * *Whose* pen is this? * *Whose* pen is good? * *Whose* house is nearby? * *Whose* car is that?

Why did she refuse the offer? * *Why* were you so cross with him? * *Why* was he so rude to you? * *Why* would you ask such a thing? * *Why* would she complain about you? * *Why* are you so late today?

How did you do it? * *How* does it work? * *How* do you plan to complete this task? * *How* are you? * *How* is your mother now? * *How* were the children? * *How* will you pay for this? * *How* do you do?

Make wh-questions from positive sentences

Sentences	Wh-questions
He can do it.	Who can do it?
Someone opened the door.	Who opened the door?
That is my bag.	Which is my bag?
She will get a certificate.	What will she get?
They want something.	What do they want?
She painted a picture.	What did she paint?
This purse is Rita's.	Whose is this purse?
She saw him yesterday.	When did she see him?
He has gone home.	Where has he gone?
She told him something.	What did she tell him?
He knows something.	What does he know?
It happened at 11 a.m.	What time did it happen?
It was his idea.	Whose idea was it?
It was my fault.	Whose fault was it?
It was her bag.	Whose bag was that?
They want something.	What do they want?

She went home.	Where did she go?
Her name is Kamala.	What is her name?
He played tennis.	What did he play?
They sang a song.	What did they sing?

Advanced Questions

What subject is he an authority on? * What university did you go? * What time did it happen? * What stop are we at? * What station is this? * What colour are those flowers? * What colour is her new dress? * What kind of music do you like? * What make is his car? * What language did she speak in? * What size shirt do you take?

Whose bag is that? * Whose idea was it? * Whose turn is it to do the dishes? * Whose fault was it then? * Whose mother are you? * Whose side are you on? * Whose shoes are these?

Which subject do you prefer? * Which train is she coming on? * Which route did you travel by? * Which side of the street do you stay on? * Which of the writers do you like the best? * Which of the two dresses do you like better? * Which of the two boys is more intelligent?

How soon do you expect it to happen? * How often has he visited you? * How fast was he driving? * How long have you known him? * How old is he? * How wide is the road? * How far is that place from here? * How difficult was it to deal with those people? * How many years have you worked with this company? * How many people were there? * How many of his books have you read? * How many pages have you read? * How much money have you got? * How much do I owe you? * How much did he lend you? * How much did you tell him then? * How much are these potatoes? * How much does this cost?

Why get upset over such a small matter? * Why ask him? Let us leave. * Why not meet him personally? * Why argue with him? * Why wait? He isn't going to come. * Why pay more when you can buy it for less? * Why hurry? * Why all the secrecy? * Why the picnic now? * He wants me to go with you – why me? Why not Ashok? * She blames you for what happened. * Why me? Why can't someone else do it? * Why so serious, Ashok? * Why so angry Preeti?

wh-questions [negative]

Who hasn't signed the register? * Why don't you tell them what actually happened? * Why don't they take interest in these matters? * Why didn't she say anything at all? * What isn't in the right place? * When wouldn't it be convenient for you? * Where shouldn't I touch? * Who isn't interested? * Why didn't you meet him? * Why aren't they helping us? * Which of these isn't yours? * Which of these is yours? * Which day you prefer to start the class? * Which one of you come from a hilly area? * Which is your favourite subject? * Which is your favourite colour?

If you don't like the way he behaves, why not tell him? * Why don't you do some walking every day? * Why don't we go out for dinner tonight? * Why not start now? * Why not wait for a few more days? * Why don't you try again? * Why don't you consult a lawyer? * Why don't you discuss these things with your family? * Shall we go for a walk? – Why not? * Why don't you discuss this some other time? * Why didn't you do it yesterday? * Why didn't they attend the lecture?

Wh – QUESTIONS FOR LOUD READING

What – questions

What sort of salary do you expect? * What are your requirements? * What happened? Tell me exactly. * What is the matter? * What is the PIN code of that city? * Well, what do you say to my offer? * What about a game of chess? * What about asking Shashi? * What about their offer? * What about giving it to him? * What about cabbages and onions? * What about mileage? * What about some brandy? * What about something to drink? * What about the pills? * What about the washing up? * What about this material? * What about this money? * What got into you? * What about this old deed? * What about this waste material? * What about this waste paper basket? * What about Thursday? * What kind of flowers did you have in mind? * What makes you think I care? * What time is it? * What's your deal? * What's your point? * What is your zodiac sign? [zodiac sign = star sign] * What star sign are you? * What's happening? * What's his name? * What do you want to hear? * What about vegetables? * What am I supposed to do about it? * What are the alternatives? * What is my monthly installment? * What is the rent for your flat? * What did you pay for the plot?

When – questions

When are we to expect you? * When are you being released? * When are you coming to stay with us? * When is the baby due? * When are you free? * When are you going home? * When are you going to Canada? * When are you open? * When are your office hours? * When can I borrow it? * When can I move in? *

When can I see you alone? * When can I take occupancy? = When can I come to stay in the house? * When can you come? * When can you do it? * When can you give me an estimate? * When can you let me take them? * When can you start? * When do you want me to attend the class?

Where – questions

Where are the best seats left? * Where are the children's clothes? * Where are the napkins? * Where are the periodicals? * Where are the public rest rooms? * Where are other bags? * Where are we? * Where are you going? * Where are you going for holidays? * Where are you located? * Where are off to? Where are you staying? * Where can I find children's clothes? * Where can I get a library card? * Where can I get Punjabi food? * Where are my visiting cards?

Which – questions

Which ships call at Mumbai port? * Which airport are you going? * Which are our seats? * Which building is your office in? * Which car shall I use? * Which corner? * Which credit cards do you take? * Which do you recommend? * Which days are best, do you think? * Which do you prefer? * Which sweet did you eat yesterday? * Which is your favourite colour?

Who – questions

Who are you? * Who asked you? * Who can say that? * Who can we ask? * Who do you think will contribute? * Who do I call in emergency? * Who do you think you are? Who do you want to speak with? * Who do you want to talk to? * Who do you wish to talk to? * Who do you wish to speak to? * Who asked your opinion? * Who do you think you are talking to? * Who gave you the right to vote? * Who gave him the book? * Who gave it to you? * Who got the goal?

Why – questions

Why are you so cross with me? * Why are you looking so miserable? * Why are you so late? * Why are you so blue? = Why are you so sad? * Why are you so rude? * Why are you so bullheaded? = Why are you so adamant? * Why do you bring an umbrella? * Why do you bring that book? * Why do you bring that file? * Why don't you behave? * Why don't you give me extra homework? * Why do you want more money? * Why did he refuse? * Why did he run away? * Why did you go there? * Why did you leave your last job? * Why did you lock the door? * Why did you pay in cash? * Why didn't he ask me? * Why didn't your brother talk to her? * Why didn't they ignore it? * Why didn't you phone me? * Why didn't you play? * Why didn't you tell me?

How – questions

How much postage do I need for this? * How close to the town hall is it? * How does it go with you? * How are you doing? * How would I know? * How are you this morning? * How is your sister? * How was your Christmas? * How is my skirt? * How do I get back to the previous system? * How do I know it? * How about a bite? = How about eating something? * How about a cup of coffee? * How about a game of chess? * How about a theatre tonight? * How about asking him? * How about asking Linda to join us? * How about cleaning up a little around here? * How about going in the summer? * How about me going to fetch them? * How about phoning them? * How about postponing the game? * How am I doing? * How are you? * How are you doing? * How do you do? * How are you feeling now?

Alternative questions

Would you like coffee, tea or milk? * Which is your favourite season, summer or winter? * Would you like tea or coffee? * Is it a boy or a girl? * Did you come by train or bus? * Was he sitting or standing? * When did you come, yesterday or today? * Who gave it to you, Ashok or Mahesh? * Did you call him or write to him? * Are you in favour of it or against it? * Are you in favour of it or not? * Do you wish to come with me or him?

Tag questions

Note: Positive sentences will carry negative tag. Negative sentences will carry positive tag.

Tag questions [positive sentences]

(Positive sentences carry negative tag questions)

It is raining outside, isn't it? * He has left, hasn't he? * You can see it now, can't you? * She likes cats, doesn't she? * You know how to drive a car, don't you? * They turned left, didn't they? * He called you a liar, didn't he? * It is very warm today, isn't it? * He was satisfied, wasn't he? * They were planning another meeting, weren't they? * You have given up smoking, haven't you? * The last bus has gone, hasn't it? * You can swim, can't you? * He will be here for a few more days, won't he? * They come here every day, don't they? * She likes him, doesn't she? * You told him about it, didn't you? * They must come, mustn't they? * Anybody can see that, can't they? * Everyone is in favour of the new plan, aren't they? * Nobody objected, didn't they? * Somebody asked you about it, didn't they? * Have another cake, won't you? * Do come in, won't you? * Be careful, won't you? * Remember to post the letter, won't you? * Have a good time, won't you? * Have a good trip, won't you?

Tag questions [negative sentences]

(Negative sentences carry positive tag questions.)

It wasn't his fault, was it? * He couldn't get the car to start, could he? * We can't do it, can we? * They don't need it, do they? * You don't feel very well, do you? * You are not serious, are you? * Don't touch the wires, will you? * Do not move, will you? * Do not forget to book the ticket, will you? * Don't forget to write to him, will you? * Don't forget to give my regards to your parents, will you? * Don't ask him to come in, will you? * Don't leave it there, will you? * She didn't have breakfast today, did she? * She has not left, has she? * She didn't help you with your work, did she? * They didn't answer your questions, did they? * You did not know I was an artist, did you? * We must not hurt others, must we? * The room is not freezing, is it? * The train did not leave the station, did it? * She is not always lucky, is she? * There is not a shorter way here, is there? * You did not break the window, did you? * You don't have any coupons, do you?

QUESTIONS FOR LOUD READING

Are you feeling OK? * Are you following me? * Are you fond of him? * Are you free today? * Are you going my way? * Are you going to eat it here? * Are you going by car? * Are you happy now? * Are you free on Saturday night? * Are you visiting hospital? * Are you ready now? * Are you writing a letter? * Are you exercising? * Are you trying to speak in English? * Are you laughing?

Is the plane on time? * Is the radio too loud? * Is the train on time? * Is there a dining car? * Is there a charge for gift wrapping? * Is there a doctor here? * Is there a drugstore nearby? * Is there a good hotel in the vicinity? * Is there a petrol pump on this street? * Is there a history of diabetes in your family? * Is there a newspaper stall nearby? * Is there a vegetable market nearby? * Is there a shoe polish tin? * Is there an umbrella in your shop? * Is there any water for drinking?

Was your car new or second hand? * Wasn't Ramesh any help? * Were the locals friendly? * Were the natives friendly? * Were there any problems? * Were you in the hotel at night? * Was your car parked under the tree?

Do you need any napkins? * Do you need anything? * Do you need anything to go with that? * Do you need it at once? * Do you need my credit card? * Do you offer short term loans? * Do you play tennis? * Do you prefer green or blue? * Do you provide short term

loan? * Do you really know the way? * Do you remember that party? * Do you play chess? * Do you have his address? * Do you have any allergies? * Do you have any coupons? * Do you have envelopes I could buy? * Do you have any homework tonight? * Do you have any identification mark on your face? * Do I make myself perfectly clear? * Do I need stitches? * Do I need surgery? * Do I need to bring anything? * Do I pay you or the cashier? * Do you have a shirt to match this?

Does that bathroom have a shower? * Does that make any sense? * Does the building have a security system? * Does the building have an attendant? * Does the conductor announce the stops? * Does the expressway go by there?

Did you hear what happened? * Do you know you were going by 80 KMPH? * Did you have a light on? * Did you like her father? * Did you like it? * Did you like the people in France? * Did you lock the door? * Did you make a reservation?

Have you had this before? * Have you had this problem before? * Have you had this problem long? * Have you heard the news? * Have you heard about Joseph? * Have you heard the latest news? * Have you lost your bag? * Have you lost your mind? * Have you lost your senses? * Have you met her?

Can I exchange the ticket for another show? * Can I fax the order to you? * Can I finish reading the paper? *Can I get it refilled? * Can I get on to the next flight?

*Can I get it gift wrapped? * Can I get this prescription filled? Can I get you a glass of water? * Can I get you anything? * Can I see the place now? * Can I see your driving licence? * Can I sell you a ticket? * Can I show you something? * Can I stay a bit longer? * Can I take a look at your paper? * Can I take it for a road test?

Could I see your menu card? * Could I sit here? * Could I speak with the manager please? * Could I talk to you sometime? * Could she come, do you think? * Could she help breaking it? * Could we borrow a ladder? * Could we have some water please? * Could you tell me what time it is? * Could you explain that again? * Could you dial it for me please?

May I have some more tea? * May I have your name and address please? * May I know your name please? * May I hold him? * May I hold it for a minute? * May I join you? * May I just finish my letter? * May I please leave the table?

* May I have a look at your watch? * May I talk to your brother? * May I wait for you? * May I see your album? * May I go home?

Must you continue to do that? * Must you dwell on the subject? * Must you repeat the same thing? * Must you keep harping on that? * Must you remind them of it? * Must I go to market now? * Must she go to school today? * Must he attend the meeting?

Shall I mention it to Avinash? * Shall I pass them to Rita? * Shall I press the starter? * Shall I send it to you or to him? * Shall I polish your shoes? * Shall I treat

the lawn for weeds? * Shall we be in time? * Shall we call on at Mohan's? * Shall we dance? * Shall we give him a treat? * Shall we go now? * Shall we call them for dinner? * Shall I invite her for lunch?

Should I take this with meals? * Should I trim the bushes this time? * Shouldn't you be at work? * Shouldn't you be in school? * Should you have to repeat it?

Will they attend the function? * Will they hold my connecting flight? * Will this compartment do? * Will this make me drowsy? * Will you ask her? * Will you be able to fetch them? * Will you be calling again? * Will you be coming around this evening? * Will you be having lunch today? * Will you be long dear? * Will you be ready by six? * Will you be using a credit card? * Will you both see him tomorrow? * Will you call at the chemist's for me?

Would you like smoking or non-smoking room? * Would you please have a taste of it? * Would you like an orange? * Would you like anything else? * Would you like bread with butter? * Would you like coffee? * Would you like fries with that? * Would you like me to bring anything?

What do you want from me? * What days would you like to travel? * What did he say about it? * What did Amar say? * What did you think of that plan? * What did you say? * What did you say the address was? * What did you think of it? * What did you think of the new house? * What did you think of the lecture? * What did you think of the show? * What did her father die of? * What did your parents think? * What do I owe you? * What do you expect me to do about it? * What do you have planned? * What do you have to drink? * What do you know? * What do you mean? * What do you need? * What do you think of my new dress? * What do you want to see? * What does this mean? * What does he do for a living? * What does it cost? * What best you can do to help me?

When is the final examination? * When is the next issue out? * When is your annual exam? * When ought we to leave? * When shall I start working? * When shall I cut the grass? * When shall I leave? * When shall I come? * When shall I meet you? * When shall we send it? * When was the last time you had a tetanus shot? * When will it be finished? * When will it be ready? * When will that be ready? * When will she be out of hospital? * When will supper be ready? * When will the school open? * When will they get back? * When is your marriage anniversary? * When are you finishing the work? * When shall I come to your farm house? * When is she going to London?

Where does it hurt? * Where does Meena live? * Where does she come from? * Where has he been all this time? * Where are they going? * Where have you been? * Where is a bathroom? * Where is a toilet? * Where is it? * Where is ladies-wear? * Where is the chocolate milk? * Where is the automatic teller machine? [ATM] * Where is the credit department? * Where is the post office? * Where do you go? * Where have they gone? * Where are you put up now? * Where is the grocery shop? * Where is your goldsmith? * Where is she learning French?

Which route would you suggest? * Which is my seat? * Which is the nearest railway station? * Which is the quickest way? * Which is his book? * Which month would you prefer? * Which of you broke that pipe? * Which one can I leave? * Which one shall I buy? * Which one is yours?

Who shall I say is calling? * Who told the boss I was late? * Who was the top of the class? * Who were you talking to? * Who is in-charge of the work? * Who would help? * Who would know about such a thing? * Who will give me a lift? * Who will help, do you think? * Who will volunteer? * Who has been eating my grapes? * Who is buying? * Who is calling? * Who is coming this Friday?

Why don't you buy one? * Why don't you go? * Why don't you go to bed? * Why don't you like it? * Why don't you ask for directions? * Why don't you make yourself comfortable? * Why don't you write to the director? * Why ever did you lose the temper? * Why ever go by the boat?

How do I get to the railway station? * How do things work? * How do things look? * How do we get there? * How do you expect me to do this work? * How do you get to the other side of the river? * How do you get there from here? * How do you like the school? * How do you spell that? * How do you want to pay for this? * How dumb do you think I am? * How far are we from the centre of town? * How long can you wait? * How long do you want me to stay? * How long does the show run? * How long is this on sale? * How is that spelt? * How late are you open today?

Idioms and their use in Sentences

An idiom is a group of words whose meaning is different from the meanings of individual words. '*Let the cat of out of bag*' is an idiom. It means '*to tell the secret carelessly or by mistake*'.

You will find below a list of idioms in English language. Study and use them while speaking.

from A to Z

= know everything about something

He knows his subject *from A to Z.*

by accident

= unexpectedly

We met *by accident* at the airport.

on account of

= because of

She retired early *on account of* ill health.

alive and kicking

= very active, healthy or popular

Even in his old age, I found him *alive and kicking.*

keep aloof

= not to become involved in something, to show no interest in people

He *kept* himself *aloof* from the people.

behind somebody's back

= without somebody's knowledge or permission

They went ahead and sold the plot *behind my back*.

hang in the balance

= if the future of something or somebody is uncertain

The future of the space programme *hangs in the balance.*

ball is in your court

= it is your responsibility to take action next

He offered me the job and now the *ball is in my court.*

behind bars

= in prison

The culprit is now *behind bars* for a long time.

beat about the bush

= to talk about something for a long time without coming to the main point

Stop *beating about the bush* and tell me what you want.

be better off

= have more money

Families will *be better off* under the new law.

His promotion made him *better off* by 1000 Rupees.

bit by bit

= a piece at a time, gradually

He assembled the model aircraft *bit by bit.*

Bit by bit the memories of night came back to me.

in black and white

= in writing or in print

I asked them to put the agreement *in black and white.*

in the blink of an eye

= very quickly, in a short time

The fast train passed the station *in the blink of an eye.*

bury the hatchet

= to end a quarrel

It seems they have *buried the hatchet*; I saw them dining out.

as busy as a bee

= very busy

Business people are *as busy as a bee.*

have butterflies (in your stomach)

= to have a nervous feeling in your stomach before doing something

She had *butter flies in her stomach* before talking to him about marriage.

the call of nature

= the need to go to the toilet

Excuse me; I have to attend *the* urgent *call of nature.*

carry the ball

= to take responsibility for getting something done

My co-worker was sick, so I had to *carry the ball.*

build castles in the air

= to have plans or dreams that are not likely to happen or come true

Come down to earth; don't *build castles in the air.*

change your mind

= to change a decision or an opinion

Nothing will make me *change my mind.*

on cloud nine

= to be extremely happy

Nowadays he is *on cloud nine* because he got admission to a medical degree.

jump to conclusions

= to make a quick decision without thinking

Think properly and take decisions; don't *jump to conclusions.*

at any cost

= under any circumstances

He is determined to win *at any cost!*

days are numbered

= a person or thing will not continue to live, exist or be successful much longer

His *days* as leader of the party *are numbered.*

turn a deaf ear to

= to ignore or refuse to listen to somebody

He *turned a deaf ear* to the rumours.

dig your own grave

= to do something that will have very harmful results for you

You are *digging your own grave* by giving out the secrets.

dos and don'ts

= rules that you should follow

Here are some *dos and don'ts* for exercise during pregnancy.

go to the dogs

= to get into a very bad state

This company has *gone to the dogs* since the new management took over.

like a duck to water

= very easily, without any problems or fear

She has taken to the teaching *like a duck to water.*

in due course

= at the right time and not before

Your request will be considered *in due course of time.*

on / off duty

= (of nurses, police officers, etc.) working / not working at a particular time

Who is *on duty* now?

What time do you go *off duty*?

I'll eat my hat

= used to say that something will not happen

I will eat my hat if he passes in the exam this year.

at the eleventh hour

= just in time, at the last possible moment

It was decided to go on picnic *at the eleventh hour.*

make both ends meet

= to earn just enough to be able to buy the things you need

Many families struggle to *make both ends meet.*

far and wide

= over a large area

They searched *far and wide* for the missing child.

feel good

= to feel happy, confident, etc.

It makes me *feel good* after talking to you.

with flying colours

= very well, with a very high marks or gradc

She passed the exam *with flying colours.*

follow your nose

= to go straight forward

You just *follow your nose* and you will find the garage a kilometre ahead.

have a free hand

= to get the authority to do what you want and make your own decisions

I *had a free hand* in executing the work.

at a glance

= with only a quick look

He could tell *at a glance* what was wrong.

God willing

= used to say that you hope that things will happen as planned and there will be no problems

I will be back next week, *God willing.*

it's all Greek to me

= I cannot understand it

She tried to explain how the system works but *it was all Greek to me.*

a heavy heart

= a feeling of great sadness

She left her children behind with *a heavy heart.*

take to heels

= to run away from somebody

The thief *took to his heels* when the police arrived.

here and there

= in various places

Papers were scattered *here and there* on the floor.

honest to God

= used to emphasize that what you are saying is true

Honest to God, Meena, I am not joking.

by hook or by crook

= using any method you can, even a dishonest one

I must complete this work *by hook or by crook.*

sell like hot cakes

= to sell quickly or in great numbers

His book on spoken English *sold like hot cakes.*

ins and outs of something

= all the details, especially the difficult one

He quickly learned the *ins and outs* of the job.

for instance

= for example

What would you do, *for instance*, if you find a member of your staff stealing?

a jack of all trades

= a person who can do many types of work, but who perhaps doesn't do them well

You may get it repaired temporarily by him; he is

a jack of all trades.

make a joke of something

= to laugh about something that should be taken seriously

Take it seriously; don't *make a joke of it.*

kill time

= to spend time doing nothing important

We *killed time* playing cards.

kith and kin

= relatives and friends

You invited your *kith and kin* for the function.

at knifepoint

= threatening somebody with a knife

He was looted at *knifepoint.*

know by sight

= to recognize somebody without knowing them well

I don't know his name but I *know him by sight.*

at large

= (of a criminal) not captured

Her killer is still *at large.*

in leaps and bounds

= very quickly, in large amounts

Her health has improved *in leaps and bounds.*

take leave of

= to say goodbye

After the meeting, she *took leave of* her friends.

at leisure

= with no particular activities, free

Let us have lunch so we can talk *at leisure.*

to the letter

= doing or following exactly what somebody or something says, paying attention to every detail

She followed my instructions *to the letter.*

at liberty to do something

= having the right or freedom to do something

You are *at liberty to act* as you like.

throw a light on something

= to make a problem easier to understand

Recent research has *thrown new light on the causes* of cancer.

within limits

= to some extent, with some restrictions

I am willing to help, *within limits.*

a little bird told me

= used to say that somebody told you something but you don't want to tell his name

A little bird told me that you are coming late quite often.

live and breathe something

= to be very enthusiastic about something

He just *lives and breathes football.*

a live wire

= a person who is lively and full of energy

Meet my friend Satish; he is a live wire!

lock horns with

= to get involved in an argument or a disagreement with somebody

The company has *locked horns with* the workers over proposed pay cuts.

lock, stock and barrel

= including everything

He sold the entire business; *lock, stock and barrel.*

as long as

= only if

We will go on picnic *as long as* the weather permits.

for so long

= for such a long time

I am sorry I haven't written to you *for so long.*

look here

= used to protest about something

Now *look here*, it was not my fault.

not look yourself

= to not have your normal healthy appearance

You are *not looking yourself* today. (= You look tired or sick or ill.)

have a loose tongue

= to talk too much, especially the things that are private

I try to avoid him because he *has a loose tongue.*

at a loose end

= having nothing to do and not knowing what you want to do

Come and see me, if you are *at a loose end.*

loosen somebody's tongue

= to make somebody talk more freely than usual

A bottle of whisky has *loosened his tongue.*

up to the mark

= as good as it or as good as they should be

Your work isn't really *up to the mark.*

in the market for something

= interested in buying something

He is *in the market for* a new car.

on the market

= available for people to buy

That house came *on the market* last week.

be your own master

= to be free to make your decisions rather than being told what to do

I have my own business; I *am my own master.*

make up your mind

= to have your opinion and make your own decisions without the help of other people

Have you *made up your minds* where to go for honeymoon?

in mint condition

= new or as good as new, in perfect condition

His motorbike is *in mint condition.*

move heaven and earth

= to do everything you possibly can in order to achieve something

I had to *move heaven and earth* to get the job.

a needle in a haystack

= a thing that is almost impossible to find

Searching for one man in this city is like looking for *a needle in a haystack.*

all at once

= suddenly

All at once she lost her temper.

plus or minus

= used when the number mentioned may actually be more or less by a particular amount

The margin of error was *plus or minus* three per cent.

powder your nose

= a polite way of referring to the fact that a woman is going to the toilet / bathroom

She has just gone to *powder her nose.*

rain or shine

= whatever happens, whether there is rain or sun

He goes for jogging every morning, *rain or shine.*

keep your shirt on

= used to tell somebody not to get angry

Keep your shirt on! It was only a joke.

show the door

= to ask somebody to leave because they are no longer welcome

He was *shown the door* for his rude behaviuor in meeting.

save your skin

= try to avoid punishment, etc. by leaving others in a difficult situation

To *save his own skin*, he lied and blamed the accident on his friend.

sit on the fence

= to avoid getting involved in deciding or influencing something

I have observed him always *sitting on the fence* at the meetings.

all smiles

= looking very happy, especially soon after you have been looking very sad or worried

Twelve hours later she was *all smiles* again.

for a song

= very cheap or at a very low price

The old books are sold *for a song.*

a square meal

= a good satisfying meal

He looks as if he hasn't had *a square meal* for weeks.

watch your step

= walk carefully

Watch your step! There are pits on the road.

have a sweet tooth

= to like a food that contains lot of sugar

Normally children *have a sweet tooth.*

through thick and thin

= even when there are problems and difficulties

He has supported the team for over ten years *through thick and thin.*

on the tip of your tongue

= you are sure that you know it but you cannot remember it

I tell you it is *on the tip of my tongue*; I am trying to remember it.

be out of touch

= to no longer communicate with somebody

I don't know his whereabouts; he *is out of touch.*

at an ungodly hours

= very early or very late and therefore annoying

Never visit any person *at an ungodly hours*; it is very much annoying.

warts and all

= including all the bad or unpleasant features of somebody or something

She still loves him, *warts and all.*

Phrasal Verbs

Phrasal verbs are a very important part of the English language. They are used in spoken English more effectively. A verb is combined with an adverb or a preposition or both to give a new meaning, for example *go in for, win over, see to*, etc.

Make a deliberate attempt to use phrasal verbs in your speech. Gradually you will come to know where and how to use them. The use of phrasal verbs shows that you have reached to a higher level of English language. Following is the collection of a few phrasal verbs for practice.

abide by

= to accept an agreement or a rule or a decision

Workers who refused to *abide by* the agreement were removed from services.

He expressed his readiness to *abide by* the decision.

account for

= to explain the reason for something or to explain the cause of something

Can you account for your misconduct today morning?

The cashier could not *account for* the shortage of money from the cash box.

aim at

= to intend to achieve something

This year our company is *aiming at* doubling the production.

One should *aim at* minimum 90 per cent of marks to pass in the IAS exam.

attend to

= to help or care for somebody

Mother *attends to* every need of her child.

A coach guard in a train *attends to* the needs of passengers.

bail out

= (1) to save or rescue (2) to jump out of the plane in case of emergency

I was there to *bail* him *out* of the police custody.

His wife *bailed* him *out* of the law court when he was arrested.

The pilot had to *bail out* because of fire in the engine.

The bomber plane was shot at and the pilot *bailed out.*

blow up

= to explode

The racing car *blew up* after it crashed into the compound wall.

The bomb *blew up* while defusing it.

break down

= (1) to stop functioning (2) to get upset

Our car *broke down* on the way to Nagpur.

The machine *breaks down* if it is mishandled.

The lady *broke down* when the police told that her son had died.

That boy *broke down* when he was scolded by his teacher.

bring out

= to release or publish something

Last year, he *brought out* the first edition of his book.

Next year, our company is planning to *bring out* the new model of car.

bank on

= to rely on somebody or something

I am *banking on* you to help me.

She *banks on* your help.

Don't *bank on* the things beyond your control.

blast off

= to leave the ground to go into space

The space shuttle designed by ISRO is ready to *blast off* in the evening.

ROHINI satellite is being made ready for *blast off*.

boot up

= to start a computer

You have to *boot up* before starting the work.

I am *booting up* to start the work.

boss around

= to use excessive authority to control people

Don't try to *boss* me *around;* I am not your servant.

Have you noticed how he *bosses* his servant *around?*

bucket down

= to rain very heavily

By looking at those clouds, anybody can guess that it will *bucket down* shortly.

We should reach home before it *buckets down.*

bump into

= to meet someone unexpectedly

Ashok *bumped into* me on the way to market.

She *bumped into* her close friend in the theatre.

bunk off

= to stay away from work or school

While in school, we used to *bunk off* to see films.

Why did you *bunk off* yesterday?

butter up

= to praise or flatter someone excessively to get the work done

I know why you are *buttering* me *up*; you want my bike for a ride.

He always *butters up* his boss to get the promotion.

buy off

= to pay someone to stop causing trouble to you

Management thought of *buying off* the union leader.

Try to *buy* him *off.* He is a trouble maker.

call for

= to need something

The situation *calls for* prompt action.

You have been promoted! This *calls for* a celebration.

check in

= to go to a desk in a hotel, an airport, etc. and tell an official that you have arrived

Please *check in* at least an hour before departure.

We have *checked in* at the hotel in the evening.

check out

= to pay your bill and leave a hotel

Guests will *check out* by noon.

I had to *check out* in the morning.

close down

= to stop doing business

Many of the restaurants *close down* in the month of August.

The factory was *closed down* because of heavy losses.

cough up

= to give money unwillingly

He finally *coughed up* the money he owed us.

He had to *cough up* the money he owed me.

depart from

= to behave in a way that is different from usual

Departing from her usual routine, she took the bus to work.

Departing from his usual route, he went through the valley.

dig into

= to find information by searching or asking questions

Will you *dig* a little *into* his past and see what you find?

Police are *digging into* his past to verify his statement.

doll up

= to make yourself look attractive for a party, etc. with fashionable clothes

Are you getting *dolled up* for the party?

She is getting *dolled up* for the function.

doze off

= to go to sleep, especially during the day

She *dozed off* while waiting for the train.

He was caught *dozing off* in classroom.

draw back

= to move away from somebody or something

He came close but she *drew back*.

The cat *drew back* when the dog came nearer.

drink in

= to look or to listen to something with great interest and enjoyment

They just stood there *drinking in* the scenery.

She just sat there *drinking in* the melodious music.

drop by

= to pay a visit to a person or a place

Please *drop by* sometime.

I will be happy if you *drop by* in the evening.

dry off

= to become dry or make something dry

We went swimming and then lay in the sun to *dry off.*

We *dried* our boots *off* by the fire.

eat out

= to have food in restaurant, etc. rather than at home

Do you like *eating out* tonight?

Today I have to *eat out* because my wife is not there.

eat up

= to finish eating all of something

Come on, *eat up* your food; we are going out.

Don't waste the food; *eat up.*

fall apart

= to have so many problems that it is no longer possible to exist or function

Their marriage finally *fell apart.*

The deal *fell apart* because of disagreement on a price.

fall back

= to move or to turn back

The enemy *fell back* as our troops advanced.

As our army advanced, the enemy *fell back.*

feel for

= to have sympathy for somebody

I really *felt for* her when her husband died.

I do *feel for* you, honestly.

fence off

= to divide one area from another with a fence

A small area was *fenced off* from the rest of the beach.

The vegetable garden was *fenced off* from the rest of the farm.

fish out

= to take or pull something or somebody out of a place

She *fished* a piece of paper *out* of the pile on her desk.

They *fished* a dead body *out* of the river.

flick through [= flip through] [= page through]

= to turn the pages of a book, etc. quickly and look at them without reading everything

I had only *flicked through* your report but it seems to be fine.

I was just *flicking through* various magazines while waiting at the dentist.

flip over

= to turn on to other side or upside down

The car hit the tree and *flipped over.*

The storm *flipped over* several cars.

fool around

= to waste time instead of doing something that you should be doing

Be serious and start doing your work; don't *fool around.*

If you *fool around* like this, I am sure you will never succeed.

forge ahead

= to move forward quickly or to make a lot of progress quickly

The company is *forging ahead* with its plans of expansion.

They are *forging ahead*, building two kilometers of road every day.

fork out

= to spend a lot of money on something

Why *fork out* for a taxi when there is a better bus service?

We had to *fork out* a small fortune on their education.

freshen up

= to wash and make yourself look clean and tidy

I will just go and *freshen up* before supper.

It seems you are tired; why don't you *freshen up*?

fuss over

= to pay a lot of attention to somebody

He was very much embarrassed at the way she *fussed over* him.

gamble on

= to risk losing something in the hope of being successful

He is *gambling* his reputation *on* this deal.

I am just *gambling* my goodwill *on* this deal.

gear up

= to prepare to do something

Dodge-ball teams are *gearing up* for national games.

They are *gearing up* for the football tournament.

give away

= to give something as a gift

Many men have *given away* all their wealth to nation.

He *gives away* lot of money to charity.

go against

= not to be in somebody's favour or not to their advantage

The court verdict *went against* him.

He would not *go against* his parents' wishes.

go ahead

= to travel faster and reach a place before others

I will *go ahead* and tell them you are on the way.

One of you will *go ahead* to oversee the arrangements.

gross out

= to be very unpleasant and make somebody feel disgusted

His bad breath really *grossed* me *out.*

The dirty clothes in your room *gross* me *out*; please take them away.

hail from

= to come from or have been born in a particular place

Her father *hailed from* Delhi.

Where do you *hail from*?

hammer in

= to repeat something again and again in order to make someone understand it

It is an important point and it has to be *hammered in.*

Children need *hammering in* for the difficult subjects.

hand over

= to give something officially or formally to another person

He handed over a cheque for 400000 INR to me.

They *handed* the weapons *over* to the police.

hang back

= to remain in a place after all the people have left

Can you tell me why are you *hanging back*?

I told them to *hang back* to clear the premises.

hark back

= to remember or talk about something that happened in the past

She always *harks back* on how things used to be in her youth.

Don't waste your time *harking back* on your past glory.

have on

= to be wearing something

She *had* a red jacket *on*.

He *has* a blue shirt *on*.

hear from

= to receive a letter, e-mail, phone call, etc. from somebody

I look forward to *hear from* you.

I haven't *heard* anything *from* her for months.

hit back

= to reply to attacks or criticism

She *hit back* at her critics in a TV interview.

She was waiting for a chance to *hit back*.

leak out

= (of information) to become known to the public

I don't know how the information *leaked out.*

The secret plan was *leaked out* to our opponents.

let off

= to not punish for something they have done wrong or give them only light punishment

They *let* us *off* lightly.

She was *let off* with a light warning.

look after

= to be responsible for or to take care of somebody or something

Who is going to *look after* the children in your absence?

Don't worry about me, I can *look after* myself.

look around

= to search for something in a number of different places

We are *looking around* for a house in this area.

They were *looking around* for a place to live in.

marry off

= to find a husband or wife for somebody, especially your daughter or son

She was *married off* to a doctor at the age of 22.

My son was *married off* to a doctor at the age of 25.

mind out

= to tell somebody to be careful

Mind out, this place is very hot.

Mind out, the door frame is low.

mistake for

= to think wrongly that somebody or something is something or somebody else

I think you are *mistaking* me *for* someone else.

He *mistook* me *for* somebody else.

pass away

= to die

His mother *passed away* last week.

Her sister *passed away*; she was suffering from cancer.

put across

= to communicate your ideas, feelings, etc. successfully to somebody

She is not very good at putting her views *across*.

He is very good at *putting* his views *across*.

remember me to

= used to ask somebody to give your good wishes to somebody else

Remember me to your parents.

Remember me to your brother.

result in

= to make something happen

The cyclone has *resulted in* many thousands of death.

These policies *resulted in* many elderly people suffering hardship.

run across

= to meet somebody or find something by chance

I *ran across* my old friend in a cinema theatre.

She *ran across* her marriage album in the cupboard.

see off

= to go to an airport, railway station, bus station, etc. to say goodbye to somebody who is starting a journey

She went to airport to *see off* her mother.

Are you going to *see* him *off* at the railway station?

shell out

= to pay a lot of money for something

He liked the house very much and he was prepared to *shell out* a large amount.

The company *shelled out* 800000 INR for the farmhouse.

slim down

= to become thinner

She has *slimmed down* by skipping the dinner for a year.

You are looking very bulky; you must *slim down*.

spy on

= to watch somebody or something secretly

Have you been *spying on* me?

He engaged a detective to *spy on* his wife.

Phrasal Verbs – Topic Wise

Following phrasal verbs are given with reference to various situations like work, travel, thinking, studying, sport and fitness, politics, health and illness, etc.

Observe carefully and use in your speech.

WORK

starting and finishing the job

(take on, take over, hold down, hand over, step down, lay off)

1. to begin to employ someone

   The company **took** him **on** as an apprentice at eighteen.

2. to start doing a job that someone was doing before

   She **took over** as office manager last week.

3. to keep a job for a period of time

   Her health problem made it difficult for her to **hold down** a job.

4. to give someone else responsibility for something

   He **handed over** the workshop to his elder son.

5. to leave your job, especially an important post

   The chairman has announced that he will **step down** at the end of the year.

6. to stop employing someone because you do not have work for them

Last year the company had to **lay off** twenty per cent of its workforce.

having lots of work

(snow under, get behind, tie up, catch up, slave away, pile up)

1. to have too much work to deal with

   We are completely **snowed under** with work at the moment.

2. to lag behind schedule

   Many of the students are **getting behind** in their studies.

3. to be too busy

   He is **tied up** for the next couple of hours but probably he may see you in the evening.

4. to do something you did not have time to do earlier

   I sometimes go into the office on Sundays to **catch up** on paperwork.

5. to work very hard with little or no rest

   She is **slaving away** to get the plans ready in time.

6. to receive more order and no men to deal

   Orders are **piling up** and we don't have the staff to attend.

dates in your diary

(fix up, set up, line up, pencilled in, squeeze in, fit in)

1. to arrange something such as a meeting

   Give my secretary a ring to **fix up** a date for meeting.

   Shall we **set up** a meeting at the end of this week?

   Have you got any more talks **lined up**?

2. to arrange something on a particular date, knowing it might be changed

   At the moment the tour is **pencilled in** for next month.

3. to manage to see something or see someone when you are busy

   He might be able to **squeeze** you **in** at two o'clock.

   Doctor could **fit** you **in** on Monday morning.

TRAVEL

starting a journey

(go out, set off, set out, heading off, see off)

1. to leave a place in order to go somewhere

   What time do we need to **go out** in the morning?

2. to start a journey

   They planned to **set off** at nine o'clock.

   They planned to **set out** at nine o'clock.

   They are **heading off** to Delhi at nine o'clock.

3. to go to an airport, station, etc. to say good bye to someone who is leaving

   The whole family came to airport to **see** me **off.**

by plane

(check in, take off, touch down, stop over, laid over)

1. to show your ticket at an airport desk before a flight

   You need to **check in** at least an hour before the flight.

2. a plane to leave the ground

   The plane was cleared to **take off**.

3. a plane to land on the ground

   We expect to **touch down** in Paris around 3 p.m.

4. to stop somewhere for a short time during a long journey

   They **stopped over** in Singapore on the way to London.

   They **laid over** in Singapore on the way to London.

by train / by car

(get on, pull out, pull in, get off, get in, pull over, pick up, drop off)

1. to go onto a bus, train, plane or boat

   The man **got on** the train to Calcutta.

2. to start to leave a station

   The train **pulled out** just as I arrived on the platform.

3. the train to arrive in station

   We are just **pulling in** to Delhi station now.

4. to leave a bus, train or boat

   I am **getting off** at next station.

5. train to arrive at a particular time

   That train is to **get in** at 11 o'clock.

6. to drive a car to stop at the side of road

   I heard an ambulance siren and **pulled over**.

7. to collect someone who is waiting for you by car

   Our man will **pick** you **up** at the railway station.

8. to take someone to a place they want to go by car.

She **dropped** the kids **off** at school on her way to work

THINKING

new ideas

(come up with, think up, throw up, occur to)

1. to think of a plan or an idea

   We **came up with** the name for our street.

   Who **thought up** a name for the street?

2. to produce or lead to new ideas

   A simple internet search can **throw up** a range of possibilities.

3. to come to your mind

   It **occurred to** me that he may need our help.

making decisions

(think over, mull over, think through, weigh up)

1. to think carefully about something before making a decision

   Please **think** it **over** and let me know before finalizing.

   It is an idea he is **mulling over** for now.

2. to think carefully about a plan and its possible effects

   Don't rush into anything without stopping to **think** things **through.**

3. to think carefully about the advantages and disadvantages of something

   It is important to **weigh up** all the different courses of action.

planning

(plan ahead, line up, set up, gear up, bargain for)

1. to make plans for the future

   You can avoid all these problems by **planning ahead**.

2. to arrange or organize a future event or activity

   We have got a series of talks and seminars **lined up** for next week.

3. to prepare for something you have to do

   The athletes are **gearing up** for the Olympics next summer.

4. to expect something to happen and prepare for it

   We didn't **bargain for** quite so many people turning up.

not thinking about

(block out, shut out, tune out, switch off)

1. to stop yourself thinking about something because it upsets you

   While writing, I tend to **block** everything else **out**.

2. to stop paying attention to something because you are not interested

   If she starts moaning about your marks, just **tune out**.

   When he starts moaning about my marks, I just **tune out**.

3. to prevent somebody / something from entering a place

Mummy, Ramesh keeps **shutting** me **out** of the bedroom.

4. to stop thinking about something or paying attention to something

   When I hear the word 'football' I **switch off.**

(= because I am not interested in it)

technology

(plug in, charge up, log in, log on, log off, log out, shut down, power up)

1. to connect a piece of electrical equipment to the electric supply

   Is the printer **plugged in**?

2. to put electricity into a piece of equipment which has batteries

   I have to **charge up** my mobile phone.

3. to type in your name, a password, etc. to start using a computer

   You need a user ID to **log in** to the desired network.

   You need a user ID to **log on** to the desired network.

4. to finish using a computer system

   Make sure you **log off** / **log out** so that other users can't access your data

   Can you make sure that all the computers have been **shut down**?

5. to touch a switch so that a piece of equipment starts working

   He **powered up** his laptop to check his e-mail.

using a computer

(zoom in, zoom out, print out, type in, key in, type up, copy in on)

1. to make an image on a screen larger / smaller

   Click here to **zoom in**. / Click here to **zoom out**.

2. to make a printed copy of something on a computer

   I have typed the letter for **printing** it **out**.

3. to put information into a computer using a keyboard

   Have you **typed in** the customer's name and address?

   Have you **keyed in** the customer's name and address?

4. to make a copy of something you have written by hand

   She has **typed up** her hand written notes.

5. to send someone a copy of an e-mail

   Can you **copy** me **in on** all the e-mails?

problems

(gone down, cut out, hack into, back up)

1. to suddenly stop working

   We cannot do anything because the system has **gone down**.

   My phone was **cut out** and I couldn't get a signal.

2. to get into someone's computer without permission

   She managed to **hack into** my computer system.

3. to make a copy of computer information so that you do not lose it

They **back up** data regularly in case of any problems.

studying

(read through, look through, skim through, flick through, pore over, look up)

1. to read something from beginning to end

   Can you **read through** this document for me?

   Can you **look through** this document for me?

2. to read something quickly without studying the details

   He was **skimming through** the reports on his desk.

   She was **flicking through** the magazine on her lap.

3. to study a book or a document carefully

   He was busy **poring over** the legal documents.

4. to look in a book or in a computer to find a piece of information

   It is easy to **look** phrasal verbs **up** in a dictionary.

writing

(take down, note down, write down, jot down, rough out, write out)

1. to write something down on a piece of paper especially so you remember it

   Did you **take down** the title of that book?

   Did you **note down** the title of that book?

   Did you **write down** the title of that book?

2. to write something down on a piece of paper

   Will you please **jot down** your e-mail ID for me?

3. to write down the main parts of an idea without showing details

   I will have an outline for the project **roughed out** by next week.

4. to write something on paper, especially in a clear or complete way

   Write out a list of questions you would like to ask.

learning

(pick up, brush up, read up on, get through, scrape through, come up)

1. to learn something new by practicing rather than being taught

   John **picked up** the language quickly.

2. to practice a skill or knowledge you have forgotten

   We have to **brush up** our Spanish before John arrives.

3. to read about something in order to learn it

   I have been **reading up on** Chinese history.

4. to manage to pass an examination

   She **got through** her final MBBS.

   She **scraped through** her final MBBS.

5. to appear in the question paper of an examination

   A question about French revolution **comes up** every year in examination.

SPORT and FITNESS

fitness and exercise

(warm up, loosen up, limber up, working out, sweat it out, work off, burn off)

1. to prepare for sport by doing gentle exercises

   Make sure you **warm up** before you go for a long run.

   Do a few stretches to **loosen up.**

   Do a few stretches to **limber up**.

2. to exercise to improve your fitness

   He has been **working out** at the gymnasium lately.

3. to exercise hard

   He is **sweating it out** on the training ground with his team.

4. to exercise to stop yourself getting fat after eating a lot

   I do aerobics twice a week to **work off** a few kilos.

   I do aerobics twice a week to **burn off** a few kilos.

team sports

(call up, sent off, play on, kick off)

1. to ask someone to play for a team

   He has been **called up** for the Indian team to tour Australia.

2. to order a player to leave the game because he has done something wrong

   A player was **sent off** for his misconduct.

3. to continue playing especially after a game has stopped

   Jones appealed for a penalty but the umpire ordered him to **play on.**

4. a game starts

   The final match **kicks off** at 10 a.m.

sporting competitions

(play off, knock out, go through, go out, crash out)

1. to play the last game in part of a competition to decide the winner

   Scotland will **play off** against Denmark for a place in the world cup.

2. to defeat someone in a competition so they leave the competition

   Anthony was **knocked out** in the second round.

3. to win one part of a competition and progress to the final

   The first two in each heat will **go through** to the final.

4. to loose in a competition so that you have to leave the competition

   The team **went out** in the semi finals.

The team **crashed out** in the semi finals.

POLITICS

elections

(stand for, engage with, stand up for, vote out, vote in)

1. to compete in an election for an official position

   She **stood for** parliament in the year 2007.

2. to show you are interested in and want to understand someone.

   We have to **engage with** younger voters.

3. to defend something you believe is important

   We need someone who will **stand up for** the rights of working people.

4. to remove someone from power in an election

   The republicans were **voted out** at the last election.

5. to elect someone to a position of power

   We will keep our promises if you **vote** us **in**.

laws and politics

(bring in, vote on, push through, step up, clamp down, crack down)

1. to create a new rule or a law

   The government **brought in** a law banning smoking in public places.

2. to make a decision about something by voting

   MPs will **vote on** the issue next week.

3. to make a plan or suggestion to be officially accepted

   The government is planning to **push through** some changes in the tax system.

4. to increase an activity

   The police are **stepping up** security ahead of the summit talks.

5. to do something to stop an activity

   The government has decided to **clamp down** on drugs.

   The government has decided to **crack down** on drugs.

problems and scandals

(back down, climb down, buy off, pay off, hush up, cover up, bring down, leak out)

1. to admit that you were wrong

   The minister had to **back down** over his claims.

   The minister had to **climb down** over his claims.

2. to give someone money so that they will not do something

   He complained that the officers were **bought off.**

   He complained that the officers were **paid off.**

3. to stop people finding out something bad

   Top politicians tried to **hush up** the matter.

   Top politicians tried to **cover up** the matter.

4. to cause people in power to lose their positions

   This scandal could **bring down** the government.

5. leakage of secret information

   The details of the report **leaked out** ahead of its publication.

RELATIONSHIP

friends

(hit off, strike up, get along, get on, knock around, keep in touch)

1. to like someone and become friendly immediately

   Harry and I **hit off** as soon as we met.

2. to start a friendship with someone

In a short time, he **strikes up** friendship with strangers.

3. to like each other and be friendly

   They **get along** well with their new neighbours.

   They **get on** well with their new neighbours.

4. to stay friends with someone, especially because they may help you

   It is important to **keep in touch** with members of the committee.

ending a relationship

(fall out, grow apart, drift apart, break up, split up, finish with, walk out on)

1. to argue with someone and stop being friendly

   He **fell out** with his neighbor and they have not spoken for years.

2. to gradually become less friendly

   They just **grew apart** over the years.

   They just **drifted apart** over the years.

3. a marriage or a relationship ends

   Thomas and Linda have **broken up** since a long time.

   Thomas and Linda have **split up** since a long time.

4. to end a relationship with someone

   Maria has just **finished with** her boyfriend.

5. to suddenly leave your husband, wife, partner and end your relationship

   I don't blame her for **waking out on** him.

Phrasal Verbs in Conversation

warnings and request

(look out, watch out, mind out, hurry up, come along, go on, hang on, hold on)

1. something you say or shout to tell someone to be careful or to warn them about danger

   Look out! That metal rod is hot!

   Watch out! That metal rod is hot!

   Mind out! That metal rod is hot!

2. something you say to tell someone to do something more quickly

   Hurry up, we are going to miss the train.

   Come along, I have to go out in a minute.

3. something you say to encourage someone to do something

   Go on Johnny, it is your turn next.

4. ask someone to wait

   Hold on, I will see if he is free on Monday.

expressing surprise

(dream on, come off it, come on, go on)

1. used to tell someone that what they are hoping for is impossible

   They will go the finals! **Dream on**!

2. used to tell someone that you do not believe them

   Come off it! You never been to Kashmir, have you?

   Come on! You never been to London, have you?

   Go on! You never been to Kashmir, have you?

on the phone

(call back, ring back, call back to, put through)

1. to telephone someone who rang you earlier

   She is in a meeting now; can she **call** you **back** later?

   I will **ring** you **back** as soon as I have any news.

   I can't answer you right now; can I **call back to** you next week?

2. to connect a telephone caller to the person they want to speak to

   I will **put** you **through** to our customer service department.

talking more or less

(shut up, speak up, spit it out, keep down)

1. an impolite way to tell someone to stop talking

   Just **shut up**, will you? I don't need your advice.

2. ask someone to speak more loudly

   Sorry, can you **speak up**? It is really a bad line.

3. to tell someone to tell you something

   Well, **spit it out**! What did she say to you?

4. to tell someone to be quiet

   Can you **keep** your voice **down**?

rules and agreements

(confirm to, adhere to, departing from, provide for, provide against)

1. to obey a rule or reach a necessary standard

   The design must **confirm to** international standard.

   All members should **adhere to** a national code of practice.

2. to be different from usual way of doing something

   The government will not **depart from** the declared policy.

3. to make plans to deal with future problems

   The plan **provides for** an annual budget increase by ten per cent.

   Many insurance companies refuse to **provide against** natural calamities.

discussions and negotiations

(enter into, engaged in, set forth, point up, enlarge on)

1. to take part or become involved in something

   The company **entered into** negotiations for purchase of the land.

   He is actively **engaged in** talks with Chinese government.

2. to clearly state an opinion, idea, fact, etc.

   He **set forth** his reasons for opposing the deal.

3. to make people aware of a fact

   The report **points up** several areas which need improvement.

4. to give more details about something that has been said or written

   He was not ready to **enlarge on** his earlier claims.

HEALTH AND ILLNESS

getting ill

(coming down with, go down with, pick up, pass on, flare up)

1. to become ill

   I think I am **coming down with** a cold.

   Both brothers **went down with** a virus.

2. to get an infectious illness

   Many patients die of infections **picked up** in hospital.

3. to give a disease to someone

   Mosquitoes **pass on** the malaria.

4. to suffer again from a disease which you had before

   His eczema tends to **flare up** when he is under stress.

symptoms

(pass out, black out, throw up, swollen up, put out)

1. to become unconscious

   My father **passes out** at the sight of blood.

   I was **blacked out** and the next thing I remember is waking up in hospital.

2. to vomit

   He looked as if he might **throw up** at any moment.

3. part of your body become larger than normal

   Her face was **swollen up** and she had a black eye.

4. to injure part of your body

   Be careful, that is very heavy; don't **put** your back **out**.

medical treatment

(care for, look after, patch up, come round)

1. to take care of someone who is ill

   She was very well **cared for** while she was in hospital.

   She was very well **looked after** while she was in hospital.

2. to give someone who is injured basic medical treatment

   We gave him a shot of morphine and **patched** him **up** as best we could.

3. to make conscious again or become conscious

   When she **came round** from anaesthetic she realized something was wrong.

recovering

(fight off, shake off, get over, clear up, heal up)

1. to get rid of illness

   She took drugs to **fight off** a cold.

   She took drugs to **shake off** a cold.

2. to feel better after an illness or injury

   He has only just **got over** a serious ankle injury.

3. an illness to go away

   Most of the symptoms should **clear up** within a couple of days.

4. an injury to repair itself and become healthy again

   If you keep it clean, it should **heal up** by itself.

MAKING AND REPAIRING

making things quickly

(conjure up, throw together, cobble together, patch together)

1. to quickly create something impressive

   She **conjured up** a delicious non-vegetarian dish.

2. to make something quickly using things easily found

   Why don't we take a picnic? I can **throw** something **together**.

   We **cobbled together** a temporary hospital to treat the wounded.

   The essay was **cobbled together** from some old notes.

   Ten people squeeze into a shack **patched together** with cardboard and a few bricks.

mass production

(churn out, crank out, turn out)

1. to produce large numbers of something, often of low quality

   The studio **churned out** a string of low budget films.

The factory **cranks out** cheap exports for the Chinese market.

They **turn out** some 1.4 million cars in the winter.

new products

(bring out, come out)

1. to produce something to sell to the public

   Microsoft is planning to **bring out** a new version next year.

2. to make available for public to buy

   The company is **coming out** with a new model next month.

repairing

(fix up, iron out, take apart, put together, patch up, work on)

1. to repair something

   He was **fixing** his scooter **up** in the back yard.

2. to find ways of solving problems

   The system is thoroughly tested to **iron out** any faults.

3. to dismantle the things and assemble the things

   He enjoys **taking** things **apart** and **putting** them **together**.

4. to repair something quickly and without much care

   Everything looked shabby and **patched up**.

5. to spend time working to repair something

He is out in the garage **working on** the car.

EVERYDAY LIFE

waking and sleeping

(wake up, get up, sleep in, lie in, stay up, wait up)

1. to become conscious after sleeping

   I **woke up** at six o'clock in the morning.

2. to get out of bed

   What time do you usually **get up** in the morning?

3. to stay in bed later than usual

   He had worked hard yesterday; let him **sleep in**.

   I usually **lie in** until midday on a Sunday.

4. to go to bed later than usual

   Don't **stay up** too late watching TV.

5. to stay awake because you are waiting for someone to return

   I don't know what time I will be back, so don't **wait up** for me.

getting dressed and undressed

(put on, fling on, do up, take off, strip off)

1. to put a piece of clothing onto your body

   He **put on** his coat and went out.

2. to put clothes on quickly without due care

   Furious, he **flung on** his dressing gown and stormed downstairs.

3. to fasten something

She has put on so much weight; she can't **do** her jeans **up** anymore.

4. to remove a piece of clothing

   I can't wait to get home and **take** these boots **off**.

5. to remove all or most of your clothes

   It was such a hot day; the kids **stripped off** and jumped into the lake.

jobs around the house

(wash up, rinse out, dry up, wipe up, clear up, put away)

1. to clean utensils you used for cooking and eating

   Leave it to me. I will **wash** everything **up** later.

2. to quickly wash the inside of something with clean water

   She took her mug over to the sink and **rinsed** it **out**.

3. to dry washed plates and dishes using a cloth

   Will you come and **dry up** for me?

   Can you come and **wipe up** for me?

4. to make place clean and tidy

   I hope you will **clear up** this mess before you go out.

5. to put something in the place where it is usually kept

   He folded the clothes and **put** them **away** in the wardrobe.

EMOTIONS

unhappy

(tear apart, swear by, get down)

1. to make someone very unhappy and upset

Each time he fell ill again, it **tore** her **apart**.

2. to show that you are making a serious promise

I **swear by** God that I will tell the truth.

3. to make someone unhappy

All the hassle over the house is starting to **get** me **down**.

happy

(cheer up, delighted in, revel in)

1. to start to feel better

She had **cheered up** a lot by the time I left.

2. to get a lot of pleasure from something

He had a talent in engineering and **delighted in** constructing models.

3. to enjoy something

She **revels in** the peacefulness of country side.

Some people **revel in** annoying others.

Single Word

A single word is used to replace a group of words. Instead of using the group of words, the use of single word will give the meaning.

example:

Antibiotic

= **a medicine that destroys bacteria**

Here the single word antibiotic is used in place of five words.

Following is the list of such words. You will study these words used in sentences.

Accomplice

= a partner in a crime

The court found him an accomplice in the crime.

Anonymous

= an undeclared authorship of a book

The identity of the author of the book is kept anonymous.

Antidote

= a medicine given to counteract poison

An antidote was given to the boy bitten by snake.

Aquarium

= an artificial tank for keeping live fish with water

We have kept an aquarium in our hall for decoration.

Accelerate

= hasten the progress or increase the speed

The runners accelerated smoothly around the bend.

The car accelerated to overtake the truck.

Assimilate

= to absorb food completely or understand something totally

It took an hour for him to assimilate the subject matter.

Annihilate

= to destroy completely

Barricade

= a barrier across the street to control the mob

The police placed barricades in the street to control the traffic.

Botany

= the science of vegetable life and plants

My neighbor teaches botany in the science college.

Biography

= the life history of a person written by another

She is writing the biography of the president of India.

Cannibal

= a man eats human flesh

Even today there are cannibals living in the deep jungle of Africa.

Capitalism

= The ownership and dominance of industry and business by private sector

America is the powerful country due to the policy of capitalism.

Carnivorous

= animals that eat flesh

By nature, the tiger is a carnivorous animal.

Celibacy

= the state of being unmarried

Celibacy is the first condition to become a monk.

Colleague

= an associate in office or profession

Will you call your colleague for the dinner?

Complacent

= a person who is satisfied with one's own achievement

I have never come across a complacent person like her.

Compromise

= a peaceful settlement of disputes between two parties

After a lengthy talk they have reached a compromise.

Drought

= an extreme weather without any rainfall

Overall agricultural produce has gone down due to severe drought.

Diplomacy

= the art of conducting negotiations and maintaining friendly relations between two nations

Healthy *diplomacy* has resulted into strong binding between two nations.

Drawn

= a game in which neither team wins

The final match between India and England was drawn.

Divorce

= legal separation between husband and wife

They are not living together; their divorce case is in the court.

Edible

= a thing that is fit to be eaten as food

Food and drugs department has approved this as an edible oil.

Eligible

= a person who is qualified for the post

He is the most eligible candidate for this post.

Emigrant

= a person who leaves one country to settle in another country

You will find thousands of emigrant Indians in USA.

Epidemic

= a disease which is prevalent widely at a particular time

The rats from British ships were responsible for the epidemic of plague in India.

Export

= sending goods to another country for commercial purpose

Plenty of oranges are exported every year.

Import

= buy the goods from another country for commercial purpose

Merchants import electronic goods for earning profit.

Eccentric

= a person who has strange habits

An eccentric person's behavior is erratic.

Flora

= the plants which grow in a particular region

Local people can tell about the flora of their region.

Fauna

= the animals of a particular region

Local people know about the fauna of their region.

Fanatic

= a person filled with excessive religious sentiments

All the terrorists are fanatics; they hate other religions.

Fiasco

= a matter ends in failure

Unplanned efforts in achieving any goal will end up in a fiasco.

Flirt

= a woman who loves men only for pleasure

That woman is a flirt; not of a good character.

Fatal

= a disease or disaster which ends in death

He met with a fatal accident and died on the spot.

Gymnasium

= a place where physical exercises are practiced

The young ones are visiting gymnasium regularly for body building.

Gravitation

= the attractive force of the earth

Sir Isaac Newton devised the laws of gravitation.

Galaxy

= a group of stars in the sky

Our earth is the part of a galaxy and there are many galaxies in the space.

Genocide

= the killing of a race

Hitler is responsible for the genocide of a race.

Glutton

= a person who is fond of eating

It is very difficult to satisfy the hunger of a glutton.

Gregarious

= the natural desire of living in a herd

Man is a gregarious animal; he likes to live in society.

Glossary

= a list of words with meanings and explanations

The glossary is at the end of a book.

Nudist

= a hermit who remains naked

Nudists don't wear clothes.

Orbit

= the path of a planet or a satellite

The orbit is the fixed path of a planet around the sun.

Obituary

= a notice of a person's death in a newspaper

I was shocked to read about his death in the obituary.

Optimist

= a person who looks at the bright side of things

I like his optimistic attitude.

Omniscient

= a person who has infinite knowledge

The almighty is omniscient.

Observatory

= a building equipped with a telescope to study and watch the stars and planets

Students visit the observatory to study the planets.

Omnipresent

= a person who is everywhere

The almighty is omnipresent.

Opaque

= a thing that cannot be seen through

His cabin is fitted with opaque glasses.

Octagon

= an eight sided figure

The administrative building is octagonal in shape.

Orphanage

= a house where parentless children are taken care of

She often visits an orphanage to distribute fruits.

Orchestra

= a body of singers equipped with musical instruments

On that day, an orchestra was arranged for the guests.

Polygamy

= the practice of having many wives at the same time

Islamic religion allows polygamy for men.

Pessimist

= a person who always looks at the dark side of things

A pessimist cannot be successful in life.

Posthumous

= an incident occurring after death

He was awarded posthumously; his widow received it.

Pseudonym

= a pen name used by an author

He used a pseudonym to keep his authorship a secret.

Perquisites

= gain or profit besides one's salary

Apart from salary he was offered attractive perquisites.

Patent

= the right to sell and make use of invention

Thomas Edison was having hundreds of patents registered in his name.

Pacifist

= a person who is for the total abolition of war

All political leaders in the world admire the pacifist.

Passport

= a document allowing permission to a person to travel abroad

I have applied for the passport to visit my son in USA.

Panorama

= a complete view of surrounding region

I enjoyed the delightful panorama from top of the hill.

Plagiarist

= a person who copies from other books

The authors had a meeting to condemn the plagiarist.

Radar

= an apparatus for finding out the position of aircraft in the sky

The enemy plane was located by Radar and it was shot down.

Revenue

= the annual income of the state

The government planned to increase the revenue by raising the taxation.

Quadruped

= a four footed wild animal

Lion is the strongest quadruped living in the jungle.

Quintal

= a weight of hundred kilograms

We bought a quintal of wheat for the marriage ceremony.

Superfluous

= more than necessary

India has a superfluous stock of food grains needed for our population.

Stable

= a place where horses are kept

Tell the servant to lock the stable door.

Spinster

= an unmarried woman

She is a spinster; looking for a lady partner in room.

Solo

= a song sung by a single person

Lata Mangeshkar has to her record 22000 solos.

Spendthrift

= a person who spends money lavishly

The youngest son of the landlord is a spendthrift.

Sabotage

= Deliberate damage to productive capacity

There was a fear of sabotage in power plant by the terrorists.

Scapegoat

= a person who is made to blame due to others

An innocent person has been a scapegoat for no fault of his.

Teetotaler

= A person who doesn't drink alcohol.

Out of the lot, there are only two teetotalers.

Taciturnity

= a person of reserved nature while speaking

You can judge a person by his taciturnity while speaking.

Tenant

= a person who stays in house by paying rent

We asked our tenant to vacate the house within three months.

Tangible

= anything that is definite and clear

People will accept your idea only if you offer a tangible proof of it.

Troupe

= a group of actors or drama artists

They have their own vehicle to take the troupe from place to place.

Tribute

= a periodic payment paid to the conqueror by the conquered

Many small princely states were paying regular tribute to the emperor.

Utopia

= an imaginary perfect place

The condition of only love and no hate; you will find in utopia.

Ultimatum

= a final proposal or warning

The government has given the ultimatum to striking workers to join the duty within two days.

Upstart

= a person who has risen into prominence from low rank to wealth

You may not believe that an upstart has occupied the chair of prime minister.

Unique

= a thing which has no equal or comparison to it

This car is unique in design and performance.

Usurer

= a money lender who charges high rate of interest

Poor farmers go to a usurer for money.

Windfall

= an unexpected fortune or wealth

You will enjoy the windfall at the end of this year.

Widower

= a man whose wife is dead

The person who talked to you is a widower.

Wardrobe

= a cupboard where clothes are kept

His wardrobe is full of imported clothes.

Waterproof

= a thing which remains undamaged by water

The truck is fully covered by a waterproof cloth to protect the goods from rain.

Verbatim

= the repetition of anything word by word

Give me the verbatim report of what you heard.

Zoo

= a place where animals are kept for show

We are visiting the zoo with our family on Sunday.

Zenith

= highest point

He has reached the zenith of his career.

Vacillate

= to keep changing one's mind

Come to a firm decision; no vacillating of mind.

Voluntary

= an action done with willingness without any expectation

Many of the workers opted for voluntary service to poor.

Simple Words to Replace Difficult Words

It is easy to speak in short sentences and it is easy to understand short sentences. It is better to use simple words in speech. Following is the list of difficult words and simple words of the same meaning. The sentences are made using both words.

Difficult word	**Simple word**
accede	**agree, grant, allow**

The opposite party has *acceded* to our proposal.

They have *agreed* to his proposal in total.

Accordingly	**so**

Accordingly you are supposed to come in line for getting tickets.

So you are supposed to come in line for getting tickets.

accustom to	**used to**

You need some time to get *accustomed to* local climate.

You need some time to get *used to* local climate.

Acquaint yourself	**find out, read**

You have to stay here to *acquaint yourself* of the facts.

Difficult word	**Simple word**

You have to stay here to *find out* the facts.

additional	**more, extra**

He had to pay *additional* money for the science kit.

He had to pay *extra* money for the science kit.

address	**tackle, consider**

To *address* a problem is to face it for solving it.

To *tackle* a problem is to face it for solving it.

advices	**information**

The necessary *advices* are dispatched for your action.

The necessary *information* is forwarded for your action.

advise	**inform, instruct**

They were *advised* to remain indoors.

They were *instructed* to remain indoors.

aggregate	**total**

Give me the cheque for the *aggregate* amount.

I will give the cheque if you tell the *total* amount.

alleviate	**ease, reduce, lessen**

Aspirin *alleviates* headache.

Aspirin *reduces* headache.

apprise	**inform, tell**

It seems they have not *apprised* you of the plan.

It seems they have not *informed* you of the plan.

ascertain	**find out**

Difficult word **Simple word**

You have to *ascertain* the availability of funds before expenditure.

You have to *find out* the availability of funds before expenditure.

assist **help**

I need a person to *assist* me in doing the job.

I need a person to *help* me in doing the job.

attain **reach**

Have you *attained* the age of 18 years?

One has to *reach* the age of 18 years for voting.

category **group**

He belongs to a labour *category*.

He belongs to a labour *group*.

cease **stop, end**

Our telephone has *ceased* to function.

Our telephone has *stopped* functioning.

Cognizant of **aware of**

I hope you are *cognizant of* your responsibilities.

I hope you are *aware of* your responsibilities.

commence **start, begin**

The test match is to *commence* on next Sunday.

The test match is going to *start* on next Sunday.

Commensurate with **consistent with**

Salary will be *commensurate with* your qualification and experience.

Difficult word **Simple word**

Salary is *consistent with* your qualification and experience.

concept **idea**

Your *concepts* are clear and hence you speak fluently.

'Your *ideas* are vague and hence you cannot do it properly.

concerning **about**

Both positive and negative aspects *concerning* the subject are to be studied.

All aspects *about* the subject are to be studied before taking any decision.

consequently **so**

The price of gold has gone up; *so* there were no buyers.

The price of gold has increased and *consequently* there were no buyers.

constitute **form**

In India, the courts were *constituted* in the year 1875.

In India, the courts were *formed* in the year 1875.

construe **interpret**

He *construed* his contract as giving him the right to do anything he wanted.

He *interpreted* his contract to act in any way he wanted.

corroboration **evidence, proof**

I knew my statement was correct when you found the *corroboration* of it.

I knew my statement was correct when you informed me of its *evidence.*

deem **treat as**

Difficult word	**Simple word**

The *deemed* university is having a medical college under it.

Our medical college is *treated as* a part of the university.

defer **put off, postpone**

The annual general body meeting is *deferred* to next week.

The annual general body meeting is *postponed* to next week.

desist **stop**

The police had to *desist* the unlawful procession of people.

The police *stopped* the unlawful procession of people.

Despite the fact that **although**

Despite the fact that you are slightly underweight, you are selected.

Although you are underweight, you are being selected.

disburse **pay**

The dividend will be *disbursed* to shareholders.

The dividend will be *paid* to shareholders.

due to the fact that **as, because**

The permission is not granted *due to the fact that* he is having a criminal record.

The permission is not granted *because* he is having a criminal record.

dwelling **home**

Dal lake in Kashmir is the *dwelling* place of swans.

Dal lake in Kashmir is the *home* for swans.

elect **choose**

Difficult word	**Simple word**

We shall *elect* the president of our society.

We shall *choose* a suitable person as the president.

emanate from	**come from**

The cast system *emanated from* the past.

The cast system *comes from* the past.

endeavour	**try, attempt**

The company *endeavoured* to expand for catering to foreign market.

The company is *trying* to expand for catering to foreign market.

entitlement	**right**

Your qualifications assure your *entitlement* to the membership of the club.

You have the *right* to the membership of the club because you have the qualifications.

envisage	**expect, forecast**

It was *envisaged* that the school admission might be full by this time.

It was *expected* of the school admission being full by this time.

equitable	**fair**

The pirates distributed the loot *equitably* among themselves.

The pirates received their *fair* share of the loot.

erroneous	**wrong, mistaken**

His decision to allow the children to the show was *erroneous.*

His decision of allowing the children to the show was *wrong.*

Difficult word	**Simple word**
eventuate	**result, happen, occur**

It is needless to say that the hard work *eventuates* in success.

It is needless to say that the hard work *results* into success.

expedite **hasten, speed up**

We request you to *expedite* the process of issuing the permits.

Looking to the heavy rush, the process of issuing permits was *hastened.*

expiration **end**

The medicine taken after the *expiration* of date is harmful to health.

The medicine taken after the *end* of expiry date is harmful to health.

facilitate **help**

The train timings are changed to *facilitate* the passengers.

The change in the timings of trains is made to *help* the passengers.

failure to **if you do not**

Failure to attend the seminar will disqualify you from the membership.

You will lose the membership *if you do not* attend the seminar.

furnish **give, provide**

He has to *furnish* the details for filling the form.

I can fill the form if he *provides* the details.

henceforth **from now on**

Henceforth you are supposed to pay entry fees.

Difficult word **Simple word**

You have to pay entry fees *from now on.*

impart **give**

Lord Buddha *imparted* his first lecture at Saranath.

Lord Buddha *gave* his first lecture at Saranath.

indebtedness **debt**

He accepted his *indebtedness* to me.

He could repay his *debt* to me.

initiate **start, begin**

He *initiated* a new system to check the late-comers.

He *started* a new system to check the late-comers.

in lieu of **instead of**

He wanted that shirt *in lieu of* this one.

He wanted that shirt *instead of* this one.

in order to **to**

I came to you *in order to* return your book.

I came to you *to* return your book.

institute **begin, start**

The college of foreign languages is *instituted.*

The college of foreign languages is *started.*

interim **for the time being**

The government has sanctioned the *interim* relief to quake hit people.

Difficult word	**Simple word**

For the time being, the quake hit people are given relief.

necessitate	**need**

The heavy rain *necessitated* the use of gumboots.

You *need* to wear the gumboots in the heavy rain.

peruse	**study carefully**

The lawyer *perused* the contract for a couple of minutes looking for a loop hole.

The lawyer *studied* the contract *carefully* to find out a loop hole.

prioritize	**rank**

The administration has *prioritized* the problem of traffic for discussion.

The administration has *ranked* the problem of traffic first for discussion.

prior to	**before**

The entire area is to be cleaned *prior to* the visit of the governor.

The entire area is to be cleaned *before* the arrival of governor.

reimburse	**repay**

Your travelling expenses will be *reimbursed* by the office.

All your travelling expenses will be *repaid* by the office.

remuneration	**wages, salary**

His *remuneration* is fixed as Rs. 50000 per month.

Difficult word	**Simple word**

He shall be paid the *salary* of Rs. 50000 per month.

render	**offer, give**

Thank you very much for rendering your valuable services.

Thank you very much for offering your valuable services.

reside	**live**

By the way, where do you reside?

By the way, where do you live?

terminate	**end, stop**

His services are terminated for his long absence.

His services have come to an end for his long absence.

supplementary	**extra, more**

It is the supplementary medicine to provide vitamins.

It is advisable to have some extra intake of vitamins.

utilize	**use**

You will utilize the funds before the year end.

You will use the funds before the year end.

Direct – Indirect Speech

Direct: Ramesh said, " I am going home".

Indirect: Ramesh said that he was going home.

Please find below the direct-indirect speech in different tenses for your study.

1. **Simple present becomes simple past**

   Direct – She said, "I write a letter".

   Indirect – She said that she wrote a letter.

   Direct – She said, "I eat a mango".

   Indirect – She said that she ate a mango.

2. **Present continuous becomes past continuous**

   Direct – She said, "I am eating a mango".

   Indirect – She said that she was eating a mango.

   Direct – He said, "I am driving a car".

   Indirect – He said that he was driving a car.

3. **Present perfect becomes past perfect**

   Direct – She said, "I have written a letter".

   Indirect – She said that she had written a letter.

   Direct – He said, "I have eaten a mango".

   Indirect – He said that he had eaten a mango.

4. **Present perfect continuous becomes past perfect continuous**

   Direct – She said, "I have been writing a letter".

   Indirect – She said that she had been writing a letter.

   Direct – He said, "I have been eating a mango".

   Indirect – He said that he had been eating a mango.

5. **Simple past becomes past perfect**

   Direct – She said, "I wrote a letter".

   Indirect - She said that she had written a letter.

   Direct – He said, "I ate a mango".

   Indirect – He said that he had eaten a mango.

6. **Past continuous becomes past perfect continuous**

   Direct – She said, "I was writing a letter".

   Indirect – She said that she had been writing a letter.

   Direct – He said, "I was eating a mango".

   Indirect – He said that he had been eating a mango.

7. **Past perfect and past perfect continuous – No change**

   Direct – She said, "I had written a letter".

   Indirect – She said that she had written a letter.

   Direct – He said, "I had been writing a letter".

   Indirect – He said that he had been writing a letter.

8. **Future tense becomes Future conditional tense**

   Direct – She said, "I will write a letter".

   Indirect – She said that she would write a letter.

Direct – The teacher told the student, "You will do extra homework".

Direct – The teacher told the student that he would do extra homework.

Direct – The captain ordered, "You will submit the papers".

Indirect – The captain ordered that he would submit the papers.

Following sentences are for practice.

Direct – He said, "I am hungry".

Indirect – He said that he was hungry.

Direct – She said, "I watch television".

Indirect – She said that she watched television.

Direct – She said, "You are smart".

Indirect – She said that they were smart.

Direct – She said to me, "You are a fool".

Indirect – She said to me that I was a fool.

Direct – He said to me, "You are a liar".

Indirect – He said that I was a liar.

Direct – She said, "I am ready here now".

Indirect – She said that she was ready there then.

Direct – He said, "I came here three months back".

Indirect – He said that he had come three months before.

Direct – He said, "Who are you?"

Indirect – He asked him who he was.

Direct – He said, "What are you doing here?"

Indirect – He asked him what he was doing there.

Direct – She said, "Are you happy here?"

Indirect – She enquired if they were happy there.

Direct – Father said to his son, "Go and pay your fees".

Indirect – Father told his son to go and pay his fees.

Direct – The judge said to the witness, "Tell the truth".

Indirect – The judge ordered the witness to tell the truth.

Direct – The captain said to his men, "Stand at ease".

Indirect – The captain commanded his men to stand at ease.

Direct – The captain said to his soldiers, "Don't return the fire".

Indirect – The captain ordered his soldiers not to return the fire.

Direct – She said to the students, "Don't go in".

Indirect – She told the students not to go in.

Direct – He said, "Let us listen to the music".

Indirect – He suggested that we should listen to the music.

Direct – The clerk said, "Let them see the manager".

Indirect – The clerk suggested that they should see the manager.

Direct – The inspector said, "Let no one touch the body".

Indirect – The inspector said that no one was to touch the body.

Direct - The general said, "Let us cross the river four miles downstream".

Indirect – The general said that they were to cross the river four miles downstream.

Direct – The hungry boy said, "Please give me some food".

Indirect – The hungry boy begged them to give some food.

Direct – The anxious mother said, "Oh! Doctor, please Save my child".

Indirect – The anxious mother requested the doctor to save her child.

Direct – The girl said, "How happy I am!"

Indirect – The girl exclaimed that she was very happy.

Direct – She cried, "I wish I were dead".

Indirect – She wished that she were dead.

Direct – "We have won a great victory", said Karan

Indirect – Karan said that they have won a great victory.

Direct – "I have spoken nothing but the truth", said the prisoner.

Indirect – The prisoner said that he had spoken nothing but the truth.

Direct – "Is Mr.Gupta at home?" asked Sameer.

Indirect – Sameer enquired if Mr.Gupta was at home.

Direct – The mother said, "Be quiet".

Indirect – The mother told the boy to be quiet.

Likely To Confuse Words

There are some words which are similar in pronunciation but the meaning and spelling are different. One word may be a verb another word may be a noun or adjective. A list of such words is given below for study and use in your speech accordingly.

Example: take the words 'allowed' and 'aloud'

'Allowed' is the past tense of allow, meaning to 'permit' or to 'admit'.

'Aloud' is the adverb, meaning 'in the audible voice'.

Both these words are used in sentences as shown under.

Loudspeakers are *allowed* till 11 pm during the festivals.

The audience was shouting at the speaker to speak *aloud.*

Another example:

Take the words 'course' and coarse'

The pronunciation is similar but the meanings and spelling are different.

The meaning of the word 'coarse' is 'rough in texture'. The meaning of the word 'course' is 'a direction taken or the way something progresses'.

See the use in sentences.

Usually a *coarse* cloth is good for cleaning the floor.

He has passed a diploma *course* in engineering.

You should be able to differentiate the words and their meanings. Observe carefully and you will come to know many such words which are similar in pronunciation but the spellings and meanings are different. You should not get confused about their spellings and meanings. If you are clear about this you will be able to use them accordingly.

ADVISE * ADVICE

Advise [verb] = to inform, to give advice about a course of action

Advice [noun] = guidance about the course of action

The teacher advised the students to study hard.

The students listened to the advice of their teacher.

APPRAISE * APPRISE

Appraise [verb] = to assess the value of or quality of things

Apprise [verb] = to inform

Banks give the loan on gold after getting it *appraised* by the goldsmith.

All the relatives are *apprised* of his serious condition.

ASCENT * ASSENT

Ascent [noun] = an act of climbing, an upward slope

Assent [noun] = an agreement

She found it difficult to walk the *ascent*.

Both the parties have reached to an *assent* today.

AURAL * ORAL

Aural [adjective] = of the ear

Oral [adjective] = spoken, of mouth, done by mouth

I am going to a doctor for the treatment of *aural* pain.

She is going to give her *oral* test of final exam.

BARE * BEAR

Bare [adj] = not clothed, only just enough

Bear [verb] = to carry, to tolerate, to give birth to a child

Bear [noun] = a large animal with thick fur and sharp claws

That poor boy was walking bare footed.

Please *bear* with me; I will attend to you in a moment.

She was not able to *bear* children.

The ice layer is too thin to *bear* your weight.

Have you seen a white *bear* in the zoo?

Bear is a wild animal living in the jungle.

BIRTH * BERTH

Birth [noun] = the emergence of a baby from its mother's womb

Berth [noun] = a place to sleep in a train

My elder sister gave *birth* to a cute baby.

I have reserved a *berth* in a train to Mumbai.

BOW * BOUGH

Bow [noun] = a stringed weapon for shooting arrows

Bow [verb] = to bend the head as a sign of respect

Bough [noun] = a large branch of a tree

The *bow* is used to shoot an arrow.

Japanese people *bow* before each other to show respect.

There was an eagle's nest on the *bough* of a tree.

BREAK * BRAKE

Break [verb] = to fracture, to split, to shatter

Brake [noun] = curb, check, control

The machine part may *break* because of mishandling.

The *brake* is applied to stop the car.

BREECH * BREACH

Breech [noun] = the back part of a rifle

Breach [verb] = to break a rule or agreement

The bullets are loaded in the *breech* of a rifle.

He is accused of *breaching* the terms of agreement.

CANVAS * CANVASS

Canvas [noun] = a strong coarse cloth for oil painting

Canvass [verb] = to visit someone asking for vote in election

Artists use *canvas* for oil painting.

He spent the whole month *canvassing* for the votes.

CENSURE * CENSOR

Censure [verb] = to criticize strongly

Censor [noun] = an official who removes unacceptable parts in a film or a book

Censor [verb] = to remove the unacceptable parts in a film or a book

The sports committee has *censured* him for his misconduct.

Any film before release has to be approved by *censor* board

Any film before release has to be *censored.*

COMPLACENT * COMPLAISANT

Complacent [adj] = self-satisfied, irritatingly pleased

Complaisant [adj] = willing to please others

He is very much *complacent* by nature.

The local people were found to be *complaisant.*

CONFIDENT * CONFIDANT

Confident [adj] = positive, assertive

Confidant [adj] = a man to whom one tells a secret or a private matter (feminine is confidante)

Entire team was found to be fully confident while playing.

She tells all secret matters to her confidant; her brother.

COUNCIL * COUNSEL

Council [noun] = authority, government, executive

Counsel [noun] = advice especially given by older people or experts

Counsel [verb] = to listen to and give professional advice to somebody who needs help

She contested for city *council* from a political party.

Listen to the *counsel* of your elders.

He *counselled* them to give up the plan.

Most experts *counsel* caution in such cases.

CUE * QUEUE

Cue [noun] = sign, signal, indication

Queue [noun] = line of people, cars, etc.

Queue [verb] = to wait in a line of people

You will answer the question if a *cue* is given.

How long were you in the *queue*?

There was a *queue* of traffic waiting for the signal.

We had to *queue* up for an hour for the tickets.

Please stand in the *queue* for the tickets.

CURRENT * CURRANT

Current [adj] = happening or being used now, in general use, flow of electricity

Currant [noun] = a dried grape

The best newspaper covers all the *current* events occurred in the country.

The *currants* are used in preparing the sweet dish.

SIGNET * CYGNET

Signet [noun] = a ring with an engraved design, signet ring

Cygnet [noun] = a young swan

The bride gave a *signet* ring to his would be wife.

A mother swan was followed by a *cygnet* swimming in the lake.

DAIRY * DIARY

Dairy [noun] = a place where milk and milk products are produced (plural: dairies)

Diary [noun] = a book for keeping a daily record of events (plural: diaries)

Denmark is the country having a maximum number of *dairies*.

You should develop the habit of writing the *diary* every day.

DEFUSE * DIFFUSE

Defuse [verb] = to remove the fuse from an explosive device

DIFFUSE [verb] = to spread over a wide area

An expert from the army was called in to *defuse* the bomb in the market.

The gas leaking from the tank *diffused* in the vicinity.

DEVISE * DEVICE

Devise [verb] = to plan, to invent

Device [noun] = a thing made for a particular purpose

The law of gravitation was *devised* by Newton.

An explosive *device* was found in the city bus.

DESERT * DESSERT

Desert [verb] = to leave someone without help

Desert [noun] = a large waterless, empty area without vegetation

Dessert [noun] = the sweet dish eaten at the end of a meal

She was *deserted* by her husband.

You will find large elephants in the African *desert.*

Many Italians eat ice cream as *dessert.*

DIFFER * DEFER

Differ [verb] = to vary from, to deviate from

Defer [verb] = to postpone, to put off, to delay

The story in this book *differs* from the film.

The court has *deferred* the judgement on capital punishment.

DISCREET * DISCRETE

Discreet [adj] = careful and cautious

Discrete [adj] = separate and distinct

You can rely on him; he is *discreet* in all his dealings.

Our city is known for the *discrete* variety of grapes.

DROUGHT * DRAUGHT

Drought [noun] = a very long period of no rainfall

Draught [noun] = current of cool air, wind, breeze

As a result of *drought* there was no crop in this region.

You will feel the pleasant *draught* on the river bank.

DUAL * DUEL

Dual [adj] = consisting of two parts

Duel [noun] = a fight between two men to settle a point of honour

National highway is having *dual* tracks with a divider in the middle.

A *duel* was arranged between the wrestlers to declare the winner.

ELICIT * ILLICIT

Elicit [verb] = to obtain, to bring out, to extract

Illicit [adj] = illegal, unlawful

The mutual discussion *elicited* an agreeable solution for both parties.

Smugglers carry *illicit* drugs across the national border.

ELUSIVE * ILLUSIVE

Elusive [adj] = cleverly escaping

Illusive [adj] = not real

Lazy men are *elusive* by nature; they avoid hard work.

Thirsty animals run after the *illusive* mirage for water.

ENVELOP * ENVELOPE

Envelop [verb] = to wrap, to surround

Envelope [noun] = a flat paper container for a letter with a flap to seal

The island nation called Ceylon is *enveloped* by sea.

She is asking for an *envelope* for posting a letter.

FARE * FAIR

Fare [noun] = the price charged to a passenger on public transport

Fair [adj] = treating people equally, just or appropriate

Fair [adj] = light in colour

We have paid the *fare* for the entire journey.

Everybody is happy with his *fair* conduct.

She is *fair* in colour and attractive.

FINALE * FINAL

Finale [noun] = the last part of an entertainment function

Final [adj] = last, coming at the end

Tomorrow is the *finale* of film awards ceremony.

You give the *final* examination with confidence.

FLARE * FLAIR

Flare [noun] = a sudden blaze

Flare [verb] = to blaze suddenly, gradually become wider at one end

Flair [noun] = a natural ability or talent, stylishness

The entire area was clearly visible in the *flare* of burning hut.

A small fire *flared* up and damaged the entire building.

She is smart enough to dress with *flair*.

She is having a *flair* for publicity.

FOREWORD * FORWARD

Foreword [noun] = an introduction in a book

Forward [verb] = to send a letter to further destination

My uncle wrote the *foreword* to a book written by me.

He *forwarded* the letter to my new address.

GILT * GUILT

Gilt [noun] = a thin layer of gold on a surface

Guilt [noun] = a feeling of having done something wrong

King's throne was having the *gilt* on all surfaces.

The feeling of *guilt* in his mind made him restless.

GREAT * GRATE

Great [adj] = extraordinary, significant

Grate [verb] = to grind, to shred, to pulverize

He showed a *great* interest in her paintings.

She is *grating* the coconut for preparing a sweet dish.

HEROIN * HEROINE

Heroin [noun] = a highly addictive illegal drug

Heroine [noun] = the chief female character in a film or story

Smugglers make a huge fortune by selling the *heroin.*

The success of a film depends on the *heroine.*

HOARD * HORDE

Hoard [verb] = to store, to keep in reserve

Hoard [noun] = a huge secret collection of treasure

Horde [noun] = crowd, gang, mob

Merchants *hoard* the food grains for earning profit.

A *hoard* was found in the cellar of a temple.

It is delightful to see a *horde* of deer in the jungle.

INGENIOUS * INGENUOUS

Ingenious [adj] = inventive, creative, clever

Ingenuous [noun] = innocent and unsuspecting

C.V.Raman was an *ingenious* scientist and his invention is named as 'Raman Effect'.

He was blessed with the best days in life because he was *ingenuous.*

INSURE * ENSURE

Insure [verb] = to provide insurance, to assure

Ensure [verb] = to make sure, to confirm

People *insure* their lives to secure the future of their dependants.

We *ensure* a good quality of service to satisfy the customers.

ITS * IT'S

Its [adj] = a thing mentioned earlier, belonging to it

It's = a short form of it is or it has (it's my pen, it's been raining = it is my pen, it has been raining)

A spring retains *its* position when the load is removed.

Now *it's* your turn to play. = Now it is your turn to play

LICENCE * LICENSE

Licence [noun] = a driving licence, permit, pass

License [verb] = to permit, to allow, to authorize

A person above 18 years can apply for a driving *licence.*

He was *licensed* to drive a heavy vehicle.

LIGHTENING * LIGHTNING

Lightening [to lighten is a verb] = reducing, decreasing, diminishing

Lightning [noun] = very quick, the discharge of electricity in a cloud

The government is planning to *lighten* the burden of taxation.

The government is successful in *lightening* the burden of taxation.

During the rainy season, one can see the *lightning* in the sky.

Human mind travels around the globe with the *lightning* speed.

LOAN * LONE

Loan [noun] = a sum of money lent

Loan [verb] = to lend money

Lone [adj] = alone, single

He has a bank loan of Rs.50000.

Banks loan the money to account holders only.

There was a lone policeman on duty at the main street.

LOOSE * LOSE

Loose [noun] = not secure, free, unattached

Lose [verb] = to misplace, to mislay, to be unable to find

The new trousers are fitting *loose* on my waist.

You may *lose* the watch if you are careless.

MEDAL * MEDDLE

Medal [noun] = an inscribed metal disc awarded for achievement

Meddle [verb] = to interfere in other's matters

He was awarded a gold *medal* for bravery in war.

He will not like you to *meddle* in his affairs.

NAVAL * NAVEL

Naval [adj] = connected with the navy of a country

Navel [noun] = the small hollow in a person's stomach where umbilical cord cut at birth

Her brother is a *naval* officer.

The belly dancer was having an attractive tattoo mark around her *navel.*

PALE * PAIL

Pale [adj] = white, anaemic, colourless

Pail [noun] = a bucket

Her face turned *pale* when the truth came out.

Fetch me a *pail* of water for cleaning the cycle.

PAIN * PANE

Pain [noun] = suffering, agony

Pane [noun] = a single sheet of glass in a window or door or partition

She suffered from a lot of *pain* when she met with an accident.

The window *pane* was hit by a cricket ball and cracked.

PALLET * PALATE

Pallet [noun] = a portable platform on which goods can be moved

Palate [noun] = the roof of the mouth, the sense of taste

Pallets are used to store and move the goods.

People eat different types of food to satisfy their *palates.*

PEEL * PEAL

Peal [verb] = to remove the skin from the fruit

Peal [noun] = a loud ringing bell, a loud sound of laughter

Oranges are *peeled* before eating.

Pleasant *peal* of bells is heard from the temple.

A *peal* of laughter was heard from the hall.

PEDAL * PEDDLE

Pedal [noun] = a lever operated by foot

Pedal [verb] = move a cycle by working the pedal

Peddle [verb] = sell goods by going from place to place, sell an illegal drug

Peddler [noun] = a travelling trader who sells small goods, a person who sells illegal drugs

The bicycle moves forward by pushing the *pedal.*

You have to *pedal* the bicycle to move forward.

He *peddles* the small goods in the city.

Police are looking for a *peddler* carrying the illegal drugs.

PERSONNEL * PERSONAL

Personnel [noun] = employee, staff

Personal [adj] = concerning a person's private life, belonging to a particular person

The *personnel* manager looks after the welfare of employees in the factory.

Whatever he is doing is purely his *personal* matter.

POLL * POLE

Poll [noun] = vote, ballet, election

Pole [noun] = a long thin rod or post

Pole [verb] = to push a boat using a pole

People are demanding the fresh *poll* to elect a new leader.

The *poles* are erected along the road side for lighting.

The fisherman *poled* the boat to shore.

PORE * POUR

Pore [noun] = a tiny opening in the skin or other surface

Pore [verb] = to study closely

Pour [verb] = to rain heavily

The doctor cuts a *pore* in the skin for the puss to come out.

It takes time to *pore* over the big book.

The dark clouds were thundering and it was *pouring*.

PRACTISE * PRACTICE

Practise [verb] = to rehearse, to go through, to prepare

Practice [noun] = exercise, use

My daughter is planning to *practise* medicine in the city.

My daughter is doing the *practice* of medicine in the city.

PRINCIPAL * PRINCIPLE

Principal [adj] = chief, main, highest in the college

Principle [noun] = truth, concept, theory

I talked to the *principal* of the college for the admission of my son.

She is the woman of *principle*; she will keep her promise.

PROPHESY * PROPHECY

Prophesy [verb] = to predict

Prophecy [noun] = a prediction of what will happen

The doomsday was *prophesied* to be in the year 2050.

His *prophecy* turned out to be true.

QUIET * QUITE

Quiet [adj] = making no noise, calm

Quite [adj] = to a certain extent

Will you keep the kids *quiet* while I am on the phone?

There house is *quite* small.

I can see it *quite* clearly.

REIGN * REIN

Reign [verb] = to rule as monarch

Reign [noun] = a monarch's period of rule

Rein [verb] = to check, to hold back, keep under control

King Ashok *reigned* for three decades.

People were happy under the *reign* of King Ashok.

The government *reined* back the rising prices.

ROLE * ROLL

Role [noun] = part, character

Roll [verb] = to turn over and over, to spin, to rotate

Roll [noun] = a long piece of cloth, paper, film, etc. that is wrapped around itself

He had a supporting *role* in the film.

The wine bottle *rolled* down the table.

Wallpaper is sold in *rolls*. * Film is wound in *rolls*.

SHEAR * SHEER (shear-sheared-shorn)

Shear [verb] = to cut off, to break off due to strain

Sheer [adj] = nothing but, absolute

The bolts holding the wheel in place *sheared* off.

It is a *sheer* waste of money on this project.

SIGHT * SITE

Sight [noun] = the power of seeing

Site [noun] = a place where something is constructed or has occurred

He lost his *sight* when he met with an accident.

We have bought a *site* for constructing a house.

STATIONARY * STATIONERY

Stationary [adj] = not moving

Stationery [noun] = writing and other office material

The speeding car has collided with a *stationary* truck.

The five star hotels provide *stationery* for writing.

STORY * STOREY

Story [noun] = narrative, a description of events and people

Storey [noun] = each level of a building

The *story* of the film appeared in the newspaper.

They are living on the tenth *storey* of the building.

TAIL * TALE

Tail [noun] = the long part at the rear of an animal

Tale [noun] = a story

I got my seat at the *tail* end of the aircraft.

She is expert in narrating *tales*.

Words – both verb and noun

Following is the list of words which are both verb and noun. The meaning of each word and its use in spoken English are shown below for your practice.

Arm [verb] = to furnish with weapons

Arm [noun] = the fore-limb from the shoulder to the wrist, arm of the chair

India is well *armed* to counter the attack of enemy.

You will be welcomed with open *arms*.

He rested his elbows on the *arm* of chair.

Bale [noun] = a large amount of a light material pressed tightly together and tied up

He was sitting on a *bale* of cotton.

Bale [verb] = to make something into bales

The waste paper is *baled* and sent for recycling.

Bat [verb] = to blink, to wink

Bat [noun] = a rat like flying animal, a flat club for playing cricket

The human eyes remain safe by *batting* the eyelids.

The *bats* rest in day and fly at night.

The *bat* is used to play cricket.

Batter [verb] = to beat violently

Batter [noun] = beaten mixture of floor and eggs for making cake

Angry mob *battered* the thief to death.

They use the ready *batter* for baking the cake.

Bear [verb] = to carry, to keep in mind

Bear [noun] = a large wild animal with thick fur.

Pillars are strong enough to *bear* the load of ceiling.

You have to *bear* the rules of the game.

Bear is a wild animal living in the jungle.

Bed [verb] = to sleep

Bed [noun] = a soft thick sheet of cotton for sleeping

When do you go to *bed* every day?

I can't sleep comfortably without a *bed*.

Bluff [verb] = to deceive by pretence

Bluff [noun] = outspoken person, blunt person

I could easily make out that he was trying to *bluff*.

You will soon come to know that he is a *bluff*.

Box [verb] = to slap

Box [noun] = a container with a lid

The stranger got angry and *boxed* the naughty boy.

Keep all your golden ornaments in the *box* for safety.

Brook [verb] = to tolerate, to endure

Brook [noun] = a small stream

The injustice should never be *brooked*.

A lion went to the *brook* to drink water.

Buck [verb] = to encourage

Buck [noun] = the male of a deer, hare

You are playing very well! *Buck* up!

The *buck* ran faster than the wolf.

Bust [verb] = to burst, to break

Bust [noun] = head, chest and shoulder cut in stone

The terrorists *busted* a bomb in the market.

The *bust* of Mahatma Gandhi is mounted on a pillar.

Butt [verb] = to interfere

Butt [noun] = the blunt end of a weapon or tool

I had to *butt* in to stop their fight.

The soldier used the *butt* to hit the enemy on head.

Chap [verb] = skin becomes rough due to cold

Chap [noun] = a man or a boy

Her cheeks were *chapped* by the severe cold.

Do you know that *chap* is a detective?

Clip [verb] = to cut with scissors or shears

Clip [noun] = a pin used to hold the hair

The gardener was *clipping* the excessive growth of plants.

Her hair *clip* is very good.

Clutch [verb] = to hold tightly

Clutch [noun] = a mechanism to connect and disconnect the engine from transmission

The monkey was *clutching* the branch of a tree.

The car needs a new *clutch.*

Compound [verb] = to mix

Compound [noun] = enclosed space

Different food grains were *compounded* to prepare the medicine.

Her mansion is surrounded by the *compound.*

Contract [verb] = to shrink

Contract [noun] = an agreement

Cotton clothes *contract* after washing in cold water.

Copies of *contract* will be given to both parties.

Cope [verb] = to be a match for

Cope [noun] = a long frock

He tried his best to *cope* up with the odd circumstances.

The young lady was wearing a white *cope.*

Crop [verb] = to come up suddenly

Crop [noun] = agricultural product

During the completion of work many problems *cropped* up.

Due to heavy rainfall a huge *crop* of wheat got damaged.

Curry [verb] = to rub down

Curry [noun] = sauce made with curry powder

He was *currying* the horse after a long ride.

I enjoyed the food along with the delicious *curry.*

Deck [verb] = to decorate, to adorn

Deck [noun] = floor of the ship

The bride was beautifully *decked* with fine dress and jewellery.

All the naval soldiers were standing on the *deck.*

Desert [verb] = to abandon

Desert [noun] = a barren land

All his friends *deserted* him when he lost his wealth.

You cannot expect a good crop from the *desert.*

Fast [verb] = to remain without food

Fast [noun] = quick, firm

As per the advice of my doctor I am *fasting* today.

The express train to Mumbai runs very *fast.*

Fell [verb] = to knock down

Fell [noun] = animal skin

The large trees along the road were *felled* to widen the road.

Poachers kill the animals to sell their *fell.*

Fix [verb] = to fasten, to secure

Fix [noun] = awkward situation

A carpenter has *fixed* the door to frame.

I was in a *fix* when that girl asked me to give her company.

Flush [verb] = (of a person or their face) to become red, especially because you are embarrassed, angry or hot, to clean something by causing water to pass through

Flush [noun] = a red colour that appears on your face because you are embarrassed, excited or hot

She *flushed* with anger.

Flush clean water through the pipe.

A pink *flush* spread over her cheeks.

Fly [verb] = to go up in the air

Fly [noun] = a two winged insect

Birds *fly* high in the sky and travel a long distance.

A *fly* was sitting on the wall.

Fry [verb] = to cook in the boiling oil

Fry [noun] = unimportant person

The cook was *frying* the chicken legs for the guests.

Don't worry about the comment of that *fry*.

Grate [verb] = to rub to small particles

Grate [noun] = fireplace

My mother is *grating* the coconut for use in cooking.

He was sitting near the *grate* for warming up.

Grave [verb] = to engrave

Grave [noun]= a tomb

The king's name is *graved* on his tomb.

A *grave* is the place where dead person is buried.

Hack [verb] = to chop into pieces

Hack [noun] = horse that may be hired

They are *hacking* the dead branches off.

During the olden days men used a *hack* for riding.

Hail [verb] = to welcome by shouting

Hail [noun] = frozen raindrops

The winning team was *hailed* at the airport.

Yesterday evening it was raining *hail* stones.

Hamper [verb] = to hinder

Hamper [noun] = sudden rush

The heavy rain *hampered* the traffic.

The *hamper* caused the traffic jam in the main road.

Hide [verb] = to conceal

Hide [noun] = skin

In rainy season the dark clouds *hide* the sun.

Boots are made from buffalo *hide*.

All he is worried about is his own *hide*. (=himself)

Hold [verb] = to grasp

Hold [noun] = the interior of a ship

Hold the rope tightly while climbing the steep rock.

The luggage is kept in the *hold* of the ship.

Host [verb] = to entertain the guest

Host [noun] = a person who invites guests for a meal

He planned to *host* a dinner for the guests.

Our *host* introduced us to the other guests.

Incense [verb] = to make somebody very angry

Incense [noun] = a substance that produces a pleasant smell when it is burnt

The decision of management *incensed* the workforce.

The *incense* is burnt in religious places.

Jot [verb] = to write down briefly

Jot [noun] = a very small amount

He was *jotting* down the main points of her speech.

There is no *jot* of truth in what he says (=none at all).

Keep [verb] = to have in possession

Keep [noun] = food needed for support

You give me only a little and *keep* the rest with you.

Whatever remains will be a *keep* for the summer.

Last [verb] = to go on, to remain for a long time

Last [noun] = final, closing

The furniture of teak wood *lasts* for a long time.

This is the *last* ball of the over.

Lean [verb] = to incline, to bend

Lean [noun] = thin

He *leaned* his bike against a compound wall.

The young man was tall and *lean*.

Leave [verb] = to let remain

Leave [noun] = permission

Why did you *leave* the door open?

May I take your *leave* now?

Like [verb] = to find pleasant, to enjoy something

Like [noun] = the things that you like

She is nice, I *like* her. * Do you *like* their new house?

We all have different *likes* and dislikes.

Line [verb] = to cover inside

Line [noun] = a row of words in a book

A coat is *lined* with a thin cloth from inside.

You will find the answer in the first *line* on page ten.

Loaf [verb] = to spend time idly

Loaf [noun] = a piece of bread

Why are you *loafing* around?

A *loaf* of bread is enough for a hungry dog.

Long [verb] = to desire earnestly

Long [noun] = not short, not brief

Everybody *longs* to have a mansion on the hill.

They are meeting after a *long* time.

Loom [verb] = to appear large and threatening

Loom [noun]= a machine for weaving cloth

The threat of the nuclear bomb still *looms* in the mind of Japanese.

Mills are using automatic *looms* to weave cloth.

March [verb] = to walk with measured steps

March [noun] = the third month of Christian year

The soldiers *marched* towards the mountain.

He promised to repay the loan in the month of *March.*

Mean [verb] = to indicate

Mean [noun] = stingy, ungenerous

I am sorry I didn't *mean* to be rude.

She is a *mean* minded woman.

Miss [verb] = to fail to reach

Miss [noun] = the title used before the name of a girl or an unmarried woman

Hurry up otherwise you will *miss* the train.

I am eagerly waiting for *Miss* Rita.

Mount [verb] = to climb, to go up

Mount [noun] = mountain

He *mounted* the stairs non-stop.

Mount Everest is the tallest mountain in the world.

Object [verb] = to oppose

Object [noun] = a thing that can be seen or touched

Many people *objected* to the loudspeaker at night.

An *object* is given to draw on a paper.

Pass [verb] = to go forward

Pass [noun] = a narrow way across mountains

Most of the candidates *passed* the exam successfully.

The soldiers walked through the *pass*.

Pelt [verb] = to attack by throwing stones

Pelt [noun] = tiger or deer skin with hair on it

The rioters were *pelting* stones at police.

Rich people keep the *pelt* as show-piece in their hall.

Pitch [verb] = to erect, to set up

Pitch [noun] = part of the ground between the wickets

The captain ordered the soldiers to *pitch* their tents.

The cricket *pitch* is 22 yards long between the wickets.

Ply [verb] = to do work with

Ply [noun] = a layer of cloth, rope, wood, etc.

The city bus *plies* from flora fountain to station.

A boat is tied to anchor by the four *ply* rope.

Pore [verb] = to study closely

Pore [noun] = minute opening in skin or metal surface

It takes time to *pore* over such a big book.

The *pore* on the surface of metal is not acceptable.

Post [verb] = to put the letter in the post box

Post [noun] = place for collecting, dispatching and delivery of letters

Will you please *post* these letters?

Please get some inland letters from the *post* office.

Pound [verb] = to beat to powder

Pound [noun] = unit of weight equal to 0.4536 kg.

Turmeric is *pounded* to powder for the use in cooking.

Please give me a *pound* of sugar.

Present [verb] = to give with love and affection

Present [noun] = a gift

They *presented* beautiful roses to their teacher.

They arrived with *presents* wrapped in coloured paper.

Rag [verb] = to tease

Rag [noun] = torn piece of cloth

There is a law to prohibit *ragging* in colleges.

You may use that *rag* for cleaning the floor.

Ramp [verb] = to rush about as if in anger

Ramp [noun] = slope joining two levels

It is of no use to *ramp* about the silly matters.

The passengers walked up the *ramp* to board the plane.

Rear [verb] = to bring up

Rear [noun] = the back part

It is the responsibility of a man to *rear* his children.

They have a beautiful garden at the *rear* of house.

Refuse [verb] = to decline

Refuse [noun] = waste matter

She *refused* to accept the invitation.

There is a vehicle to collect the *refuse* in the city.

Ring [verb] = to cause a bell to sound

Ring [noun] = a ring worn in finger

The bells were *ringing* in temple.

She was wearing a diamond *ring.*

Rock [verb] = to move gently to and fro

Rock [noun] = a large stone

Gentle hands of caring mother *rock* the cradle.

A huge *rock* rolled down the mountain.

Scale [verb] = to climb

Scale [noun] = series of marks on rule for measuring

Who is the first woman to *scale* the Mount Everest?

How much does it read on the *scale*?

Settle [verb] = to decide, to agree

Settle [noun] = a wooden bench with a high back and arms

There is a pressure on the union to *settle* the dispute.

She was relaxing on the *settle* in the garden.

Shed [verb] = to let something fall or flow

Shed [noun] = roofed shelter used as store

Trees *shed* the leaves in winter.

The extra furniture is kept in the *shed.*

Slip [verb] = to slide accidentally

Slip [noun] = a small mistake

She *slipped* on the muddy slope.

He sang the whole poem without making a single *slip.*

Excuse me it was a *slip* of tongue.

Soil [verb] = to become dirty

Soil [noun] = upper layer of earth

His hands got *soiled* while working in the field.

Farmers till the land to make the *soil* loose for sowing.

Sow [verb] = to plant seeds

Sow [noun] = fully grown female pig

The land is tilled before *sowing*.

The little girl was scared of the *sow* in the yard.

Spot [verb] = to become marked with spots

Spot [noun] = small round mark

The desk is *spotted* with ink spilt by students.

She is having a beauty *spot* on her chin.

State [verb] = to say clearly

State [noun] condition

What he *stated* is absolutely correct.

Oh! What a pitiable *state* of affairs!

Stay [verb] = to remain

Stay [noun] = a rope supporting a pole

The cat *stayed* out all night.

Lamp posts are tied with *stays* to keep them vertical.

Suit [verb] = to adapt

Suit [noun] = set of clothes worn together

You may join our company if it *suits* you.

He was wearing a costly *suit* on his marriage day.

Take [verb] = to get hold of

Take [noun] = amount of money taken

I forgot to *take* my bag with me when I got off the bus.

What is your *take* home salary?

Tear [verb] = to split

Tear [noun] = a drop of liquid falling from the eyes

She was *tearing* the cloth into pieces.

The *tears* were dropping from her eyes while weeping.

Till [verb] = to cultivate the land

Till [noun] = a box for money on the counter

A farmer has to *till* the land before sowing.

Shop owners keep the cash collected in the *till.*

Toll [verb] = to ring a bell slowly at regular intervals

Toll [noun] = tax for using road, bridge, etc.

The church bell *tolled* on Sunday.

Motorists have to pay the *toll* for using the new bridge.

Tot [verb] = to add, to total

Tot [noun] = a young kid

Tot up the expenditure on the construction of shed.

There is a school nearby for the tiny *tots.*

Wage [verb] = to carry on, to engage in

Wage [noun] = payment for work done

British army *waged* a war with French army in India.

She was paid her *wages* in the evening.

Synonyms and Antonyms

Synonym = a word of the same meaning

Antonym = a word of the opposite meaning

The list of synonyms and antonyms is given below. The main words are used in sentences. You write down your own sentences.

(Syn = Synonym and Ant = antonym)

Adversary [noun]

Syn: enemy, opponent, rival, competitor

Ant: ally, helper, assistant, partner, friend, aid

Shivaji was the strong adversary to Aurangzeb.

Vicinity [noun]

Syn: nearness, proximity, locality, closeness, area

Ant: extent, span, remoteness, farness

There was a heavy rain in the vicinity.

Confront [verb]

Syn: face, challenge, oppose, resist

Ant: avoid, elude, dodge, foil, evade, shun

The problems that confront us are drought and poverty.

Repose [verb]

Syn: rest, sleep, ease, calm, trust, place

Ant: work, toil, support, irritate, mistrust

Everybody was reposing after the exhaustive work.

Cater [verb]

Syn: provide, furnish, supply, satisfy, pamper

Ant: deprive, stop, check, prevent

Most of our work now involves catering for weddings.

Captive [adj]

Syn: imprisoned, confined, enslaved, caged

Ant: free, liberated, at large, loose

Japanese soldiers were held captive during the war.

Affection [noun]

Syn: love, fondness, attachment, devotion, goodwill

Ant: hatred, animosity, antipathy, malice

Naturally mother has great affection towards her child.

Inclement [adj]

Syn: cruel, severe, harsh, stormy, merciless, pitiless

Ant: mild, soft, kind, merciful, generous, pitiful

Mountaineers face inclement weather while climbing.

Ruthless [adj]

Syn: cruel, merciless, atrocious, savage, brutal

Ant: kind, generous, merciful, tender, cordial

The police had to be ruthless in controlling the mob.

Illustrious [adj]

Syn: ideal, eminent, celebrated, famous, exalted

Ant: lowly, mean, poor, humble, meek, spiritless

Subhash Bose was an illustrious leader who opposed British in India.

Terrible [adj]

Syn: harmful, awful, dreadful, fearful, frightful

Ant: harmless, feeble, weak, pleasant, fearless

We had a terrible experience on that rainy night.

Complacent [adj]

Syn: self-satisfied, smug, assured, pleased, contented

Ant: displeased, discontented, churlish, grumbling

Everybody knows that she is very much complacent.

Cozy [adj]

Syn: comfortable, convenient, pleasant, happy

Ant: uncomfortable, unhappy, inconvenient, painful

I hope our guest is cozy in that hotel.

Vehemently [adj]

Syn: strongly, eagerly, fiercely, powerfully, ardently

Ant: moderately, humbly, controllably, masterly

The brave boy fought vehemently with those thieves.

Flair [noun]

Syn: aptitude, talent, ability, smartness, keenness

Ant: dullness, stupidity, idiocy, sluggishness

She is an actress and naturally she is having the flair for publicity.

Inordinate [adj]

Syn: excessive, uncontrolled, unregulated, disorderly

Ant: moderate, depleted, regular, controlled, scanty

I regret for the inordinate delay in my response.

Flatter [verb]

Syn: cajole, praise, laud, exalt, please, coax, entice

Ant: denounce, condemn, displease, insult

You need not flatter me for getting your work done.

Misfortune [noun]

Syn: bad luck, calamity, disaster, adversity, mishap

Ant: good luck, prosperity, success, fortune, boon

I faced the misfortune of serious illness.

Stimulate [verb]

Syn: excite, instigate, incite, rouse, kindle, inspire

Ant: deter, discourage, prevent, warn, scare, terrify

The chief guest was present on the ground to stimulate the players.

Calamity [noun]

Syn: disaster, misfortune, distress, harm, adversity

Ant: prosperity, success, boon, welfare, comfort

The entire region is affected by the calamity of draught.

Sturdy [adj]

Syn: strong, robust, firm, hardy, powerful, durable

Ant: weak, infirm, feeble, fragile, delicate, flimsy

That motorbike is sturdy and attractive.

Incredible [adj]

Syn: unbelievable, impossible, wonderful, unreliable

Ant: believable, credible, reliable, plausible, tenable

I heard his incredible story of sea voyage.

Flexible [adj]

Syn: yielding, pliable, bending, supple, adaptable

Ant: inflexible, stiff, unbending, unyielding, rigid

You need to be flexible in dealing with your tenants.

Pandemonium [noun]

Syn: uproar, tumult, bedlam, chaos, confusion

Ant: quiet, peace, tranquility, calm, serenity, silence

The entire assembly hall was in pandemonium.

Authentic [adj]

Syn: genuine, true, original, real, sure, credible

Ant: false, spurious, baseless, fictitious

You have to submit the authentic documents for getting the PAN card.

Tedious [adj]

Syn: tiresome, wearisome, irksome, soporific, tardy

Ant: light, cheery, charming, fascinating, enthralling

Our journey to dam site was quite tedious because of no good road.

Lethal [adj]

Syn: fatal, harmful, deadly, poisonous, noxious

Ant: harmless, safe, non-toxic, inoffensive

The thief was hiding a lethal weapon in his sleeve.

Abridge [verb]

Syn: shorten, cut, short, curtail, reduce, diminish

Ant: enlarge, extend, increase, expand, add

You will get the abridged edition of this book.

Numinous [adj]

Syn; supernatural, divine, heavenly, supreme

Ant: human, worldly, earthly, natural, living

Swamy Vivekanand was blessed with numinous powers.

Revoke [verb]

Syn: repeal, cancel, take back, withdraw, nullify

Ant: confirm, approve, affirm, sanction, validate

His promotion was revoked for the unknown reason.

Novelty [noun]

Syn: newness, modernity, originality, freshness

Ant: staleness, insipidness, commonness

You try this shirt, it is a novelty item.

Meticulous [adj]

Syn: careful, exact, precise, fastidious, scrupulous

Ant: careless, sloppy, casual, unscrupulous, forgetful

He is very much meticulous in all activities.

Conceal [verb]

Syn: hide, cover, mask, seal, veil, disguise

Ant: uncover, expose, reveal, open, unveil, disclose

It was found out that a lot of information was concealed.

Intervention [noun]

Syn: interference, intrusion, intercession, mediation

Ant: assistance, aid, help, support, favour

I was terribly upset by the intervention of outsiders.

Perturb[verb]

Syn: disturb, disquiet, trouble, anger, annoy

Ant: pacify, endure, repress, compose, silence

Don't be perturbed by his comments; take it lightly.

Dogma [noun]

Syn: principle, doctrine, opinion, creed, maxim

Ant: unbelief, falsehood, disbelief, skepticism

Certain dogmas are to be accepted without doubt.

Adulterate [verb]

Syn: debase, corrupt, pollute, contaminate, defile

Ant: purify, cleanse, clean, wash, refine, distil, filter

Government has appointed an officer to check the adulterated eatables.

Frustrate [verb]

Syn: foil, upset, disappoint, confound, hinder, mar

Ant: encourage, abet, support, succor, accomplish

He is frustrated for his failure in the examination.

Unanimous [adj]

Syn: agreed, accordant, suitable, apt, compatible

Ant: disagreed, different, variant, quarrelsome

The doctors were unanimous about the treatment to the patient.

Inevitable [adj]

Syn: unavoidable, ineludible, necessary, irresistible

Ant: avoidable, uncertain, doubtful, casual

It was inevitable for me to attend the conference.

Stimulation [noun]

Syn: encouragement, awakening, provocation

Ant: abatement, conciliation, mitigation

The stimulation is necessary for children to take part in games.

Negligent [adj]

Syn: careless, inattentive, neglectful, dreamy

Ant: careful, attentive, watchful, alert, vigilant

It was my mistake to depend on that negligent person.

Parasite [noun]

Syn: sycophant, hanger on, flatterer, truckler, slave

Ant: master, ruler, leader, director, blusterer

That political leader is surrounded by parasites.

Eloquent [adj]

Syn: fluent, glib, articulate, expressive, cogent

Ant: hesitant, silent, stupid, sluggish, reticent

The audience was highly impressed by her eloquent speech.

Spasmodic [adj]

Syn: sporadic, intermittent, occasional, jerky, erratic

Ant: regular, continuous, continual, constant

I am getting spasmodic pain in my stomach; I have to consult my doctor.

Reluctant [adj]

Syn: unwilling, disinclined, opposed, averse

Ant: willing, inclined, eager, ready, sedulous

I could make out that you were reluctant to join us in meeting.

Latent [adj]

Syn: hidden, invisible, concealed, dormant, secret

Ant: obvious, evident, implicit, unperceived

Man is unaware of the latent power in his brain.

Inscrutable [adj]

Syn: mysterious, hidden, unfathomable, secret

Ant: plain, clear, obvious, pellucid, lucid, evident

Meditation will develop inscrutable power in the brain of a man.

Mockery [noun]

Syn: ridicule, satire, sarcasm, imitation, derision

Ant: respect, honour, praise, flattery, appreciation

The local kids enjoyed in the mockery of old man.

Aggravate [verb]

Syn: worsen, increase, annoy, enrage, tease, irritate

Ant: mitigate, lessen, minimize, pacify, compose

Do not aggravate the situation by laughing at them.

Exotic [adj]

Syn: not native, unusual, strange, exciting, striking

Ant: native, natural, inborn, intrinsic, original

They could see many exotic places during the European tour.

Entreat [verb]

Syn: request, solicit, implore, ask, supplicate, crave

Ant: compel, order, command, demand, force, rob

He entreated her to accompany him to planetarium.

Untidy [adj]

Syn: dirty, unclean, soiled, filthy, polluted, nasty

Ant: tidy, clean, decent, unstained, untarnished

He wore untidy dress in the last evening.

Violate [verb]

Syn: break, transgress, disregard, disobey, infringe

Ant: observe, obey, follow, respect, regard, execute

Employment of children violates human rights.

Thrift [noun]

Syn: economy, saving, frugality, miserliness

Ant: waste, lavishness, wastefulness, prodigality

You have to practice thrift while spending money on big projects.

Delectable [adj]

Syn: enjoyable, pleasant, delightful, palatable

Ant: nauseous, offensive, repulsive, unpalatable

She was very much pleased with the delectable dinner.

Profound [adj]

Syn: deep, great, intense, extreme, sagacious

Ant: shallow, light, erratic, simple, silly, superficial

Undoubtedly he has a profound knowledge of the subject.

Provoke [verb]

Syn: incite, stimulate, arouse, induce, infuriate

Ant: pacify, soothe, placate, cheer, please, alleviate

He is a man of short temper; he is dangerous if provoked.

Industrious [adj]

Syn: diligent, busy, active, sedulous, labourious

Ant: inactive, indolent, idle, slack, lazy, slothful

He dislikes wasting time; he is as industrious as an ant.

Regretful [adj]

Syn: sorrowful, repentant, painful, worried, vexed

Ant: satisfied, contented, remorseless, cheerful

They were regretful about their hasty decision

Ridiculous [adj]

Syn: absurd, funny, comic, laughable, foolish, odd

Ant: serious, grave, rational, reasonable

I was surprised to know his ridiculous suggestion.

Cumbersome [adj]

Syn: burdensome, awkward, difficult, encumbering

Ant: light, sandy, loose, buoyant

No porter was ready to carry that cumbersome luggage.

Immaculate [adj]

Syn: pure, faultless, innocent, clean, neat, spotless

Ant: impure, unclean, faulty, tainted, stained

His service record was immaculate and appreciable.

Denounce [verb]

Syn: condemn, criticize, accuse, blame, impeach

Ant: praise, applaud, commend, appreciate, glorify

British government denounced him as a traitor.

Prerogative [noun]

Syn: privilege, right, power, choice, claim, liberty

Ant: overriding, dominance, violation, infringement

It is your prerogative to select your team members.

Swallow [verb]

Syn: gulp, engulf, assimilate, absorb, consume

Ant: vomit, spew, expel, discharge, puke, throw up

The patient swallowed the bitter medicine.

Prosperous [adj]

Syn: rich, wealthy, affluent, thriving, fortunate

Ant: unfortunate, unsuccessful, poor, needy

The hard working persons will be prosperous in life.

Tremulous [adj]

Syn: trembling, nervous, timid, shivering, uncertain

Ant: steady, firm, safe, balanced, imperturbable

That old man was begging with the tremulous hand.

Vanish [verb]

Syn: disappear, depart, evaporate, fade

Ant: appear, emerge, arise, surface, be visible

I saw the thief vanishing into darkness.

Profuse [adj]

Syn: abundant, lavish, plentiful, overflowing

Ant: scarce, scanty, meager, inadequate, limited

The doctor stopped the profuse bleeding by dressing the wound.

Accomplish [verb]

Syn: carryout, perform, finish, complete, attain

Ant: fail, deter, undo, nullify, forsake, relinquish

He could accomplish the task purely by his hard work.

Sophisticated [adj]

Syn: refined, polished, knowledgeable, not naive

Ant: naive, simple, artless, ingenuous

Anybody will be highly impressed by his sophisticated manners.

Staunch [adj]

Syn: firm, steadfast, strong, loyal, substantial

Ant: shaky, disloyal, infidel, weak, treacherous

He is a staunch supporter of the republican party.

Fanciful [adj]

Syn: romantic, whimsical, fantastic, freakish

Ant: sincere, serious, resolute, steady, reasonable

It is very difficult to satisfy a fanciful person.

Debility [noun]

Syn: weakness, infirmity, feebleness, lassitude

Ant: strength, power, energy, potency, force

Due to long sickness, he is suffering from debility.

Reiterate [verb]

Syn: repeat, reproduce, recite, renew, recapitulate

Ant: retract, cancel, revoke, withdraw, abjure

He reiterated the same old story of his trip to Europe.

Paramount [adj]

Syn: supreme, eminent, excellent, superior, unique

Ant: common, inferior, lesser, smallest, subordinate

Honesty is of paramount importance in any field of activity.

Zenith [noun]

Syn: top, pinnacle, climax, apex, maximum, summit

Ant: base, lowest point, bottom, foot, minimum

He had reached the zenith of his illustrious career.

Diminish [verb]

Syn: reduce, trim, decrease, curtail, minimize

Ant: increase, enlarge, extend, expand, dilate, swell

Take this medicine; your pain will diminish.

Chastise [verb]

Syn: punish, castigate, reprimand, afflict, discipline

Ant: reward, encourage, promote, cheer, succor

The disobedient servant was chastised for his grave mistake.

Candid [adj]

Syn: frank, outspoken, open, just, honest, impartial

Ant: crafty, tricky, shrewd, foxy, cunning

He offered his candid comments on the sports competition.

Inception [noun]

Syn: start, beginning, origin, inauguration, opening,

Ant: end, close, finish, complete

Continuous improvement is observed since the inception of industry.

Bellicose [adj]

Syn: warlike, quarrelsome, belligerent, aggressive

Ant: peaceful, pacific, placid, submissive, mild

People avoid him for his bellicose attitude.

Stagnant [adj]

Syn: inactive, dull, inert, motionless, standing

Ant: flowing, active, lively, running, teeming

Stagnant water is very dirty.

Distrortion [noun]

Syn: deformation, disfigure, deformity, misshape

Ant: beauty, grace, loveliness, adornment

Modern metal alloy is resistant to distortion and wear.

Doctrine [noun]

Syn: principle, dogma, belief, faith, creed, opinion

Ant: disbelief, falsehood, infidelity, incredulity

Each political party has its own doctrine to follow.

Splendid [adj]

Syn: grand, magnificent, excellent, gorgeous, best

Ant: dull, dim, dark, dismal, gloomy, insipid, murky

We enjoyed a splendid holiday on the island.

Ferocious [adj]

Syn: cruel, brutal, savage, violent, murderous

Ant: gentle, merciful, mild, tender, meek, docile

The forest guards set up a trap to catch the ferocious tiger.

Erratic [adj]

Syn: improper, unreliable, irregular, unstable

Ant: steady, proper, reliable, regular, stable, firm

Eradicate [verb]

Syn: uproot, pull up, eliminate, exterminate, kill

Ant: implant, embed, confirm, protect, save, settle

The labour ministry is planning to eradicate the unemployment problem.

Exaggerate [verb]

Syn: overstate, magnify, increase, enlarge, inflate

Ant: understate, lessen, shrink, diminish

It appears you are exaggerating the case; I can't believe it.

Shrewd [adj]

Syn: clever, intelligent, wise, astute, crafty, careful

Ant: foolish, stupid, ignorant, absurd, senseless

He is successful in his career because he is shrewd.

Consistency [noun]

Syn: firmness, coherence, uniformity, steadfastness

Ant: variance, incoherence, incompatibility

You are successful due to consistency in your efforts.

Thrive[verb]

Syn: prosper, flourish, grow, succeed, attain, achieve

Ant: lose, ruin, miss, squander, forfeit, deprive

He is having a thriving business of diamonds in town.

Incriminate [verb]

Syn: accuse, charge, indict, impeach, entangle

Ant: exonerate, exculpate, acquit, uphold, justify

He was incriminated for the misuse of society funds.

Delicious [adj]

Syn: very tasty, palatable, delightful, pleasing

Ant: bitter, sour, unpalatable, distasteful, unpleasing

She was very much happy to have a delicious dinner.

Admonition[noun]

Syn: reproof, rebuke, reprimand, reproach, caution

Ant: approval, praise, flattery, cajole, encomium

The student got the admonition for his misconduct.

Wrangle [verb]

Syn: quarrel, dispute, argue, squabble, brawl

Ant: agree, accord, confirm, suit, accede

India and Pakistan are wrangling over the Kashmir issue since last 60 years.

Exonerate [verb]

Syn: acquit, free, release, exculpate, pardon, excuse

Ant: accuse, convict, incriminate, impute, indict

He is exonerated by the court of law.

Vindictive [adj]

Syn: revengeful, malicious, punitive, spiteful

Ant: merciful, gracious, kind, generous, lenient

She is well known for her vindictive nature.

Canard [noun]

Syn: scandal, rumour, hoax, story, hearsay

Ant: truth, fact, reality, accuracy, exactness

Somebody is deliberately spreading the canard to defame me.

Adequate [adj]

Syn: sufficient, enough, ample, suitable

Ant: insufficient, unfit, unsuitable, incompetent

You will be provided the adequate food while on duty.

Proscribe [verb]

Syn: forbid, condemn, denounce, prohibit, restrict

Ant: invite, welcome, entreat, implore, praise

Government is declaring the proscribed organizations.

Colossal [adj]

Syn: huge, immense, enormous, mammoth, gigantic

Ant: tiny, miniature, minute, microscopic, little

The royal palace of England is colossal and worth seeing.

Inadvertent [adj]

Syn: careless, negligent, inattentive, unintentional

Ant: careful, attentive, sincere, intentional, planned

I regret for the inadvertent delay in replying.

Adamant [adj]

Syn: unyielding, firm, stern, obstinate, stubborn

Ant: yielding, flexible, submissive, docile, adaptable

Sunita is very much adamant by nature.

Decimate [verb]

Syn: destroy, kill, ruin, devastate, eliminate, nullify

Ant: build up, create, establish, generate, install

When locusts attack the field they almost decimate the crop.

Mansion [noun]

Syn: castle, palace, villa, stately, home

Ant: hut, cottage, outhouse, cabin, shack

The mansion on the top of the hill belongs to the royal family.

Crass [adj]

Syn: stupid, foolish, boorish, unrefined, insane

Ant: sane, wise, refined, sensitive, smart, polished

There is no point in arguing with that crass fellow.

Sluggish [adj]

Syn: inactive, lazy, idle, tardy, low, slow moving

Ant: industrious, labourious, active, busy, diligent

She was complaining about her sluggish partner.

Lucrative [adj]

Syn: profitable, remunerative, paying, well paid

Ant: unprofitable, useless, worthless, valueless

She is offered a service with a lucrative salary.

Pragmatic [adj]

Syn: dogmatic, practical, realistic, sensible, active

Ant: impractical, idealistic, unworkable, wild

He is the most pragmatic person I have come across.

Inferno [noun]

Syn: hell, abyss, agony, ordeal, torment, a large fire

Ant: heaven, paradise, utopia, ecstasy, bliss

The fire fighters were struggling hard to bring the inferno under control.

Stalemate [noun]

Syn: deadlock, impasse, standstill, tie

Ant: progress, development

The discussion on the border issue with Burma is in stalemate.

Prattle [noun]

Syn: idle talk, babble, chat, gossip, rumour

Ant: silence, calm, muteness, quiet, taciturnity

You will go mad if you listen to their prattle.

Fiasco [noun]

Syn: failure, flop, mess, fizzle, collapse, catastrophe

Ant: success, prosperity, progress, victory

Hitler's dream of ruling the world ended in a fiasco.

Condone [verb]

Syn: forgive, overlook, excuse, exonerate, pass

Ant: punish, retaliate, avenge, condemn, castigate

His failure was condoned and he was declared pass.

Animosity [noun]

Syn: enmity, hatred, aversion, antipathy, acrimony

Ant: love, affection, fondness, warmth

The rivals in boxing game felt great animosity towards each other.

Repulsive [adj]

Syn: disgusting, unpleasant, horrible, repellant

Ant: pleasing, agreeable, attractive, superb

The audience did not approve of his repulsive attitude.

Imprecation [noun]

Syn: curse, abuse, denunciation, vituperation

Ant: blessing, grace, invocation, honour

She is suffering from the imprecation of that old woman.

Pauper [noun]

Syn: poor person, beggar, insolvent, bankrupt

Ant: rich person, solvent, wealthy person

My brother gave Rs. 100 to the pauper in the market.

Idiomatic Comparisons – Simile

Simile is a figure of speech in which *one thing is compared to another.* When a direct comparison is made between two objects of different kinds which have at least one point in common, it is called *simile.*

You will find below the use of idiomatic comparisons in the speech. These can be used in our speech as and when the situation demands. You try to write your own sentences using the idioms.

as ageless as the sun

The earth we live on is as ageless as the sun.

as ambitious as the devil

Hitler of Germany wanted to rule the globe; he was as ambitious as the devil.

as afraid as a grasshopper

His brother is timid; he is as afraid as a grasshopper.

as agile as a cat

All the boys doing the gymnastics are as agile as a cat.

as active as quicksilver

The pilot of a plane has to be as active as quicksilver.

as bald as an egg

The cancer patient's head is as bald as an egg.

as bashful as a schoolgirl

She is beautiful; she is as bashful as a schoolgirl.

as big as an elephant

The bull in the market was as big as an elephant.

as black as coal

The buffalo's colour is as black as coal.

as black as midnight

There was a power failure in Metro station and it was as black as midnight.

as blind as a bat

That boy has lost his vision; he is as blind as a bat.

as busy as a bee

She doesn't waste time; she is as busy as a bee.

as brittle as glass

The china made saucers are as brittle as glass.

as bright as a day

The ground was flooded with lights and it was as bright as a day.

as brief as a dream

My European tour was very short; it was as brief as a dream.

as brave as a lion

In Mahabharat war, Bheema was as brave as a lion.

as brainless as a chimpanzee

Some uneducated men are as brainless as a chimpanzee.

as boundless as the ocean

Sahara desert is very large; as boundless as the ocean.

as cautious as a fox

One has to be careful and be as cautious as a fox.

as changeable as a weather-cock.

Many people are weak minded and their thoughts are as changeable as a weather-cock.

as cheap as dirt

The yield of onion crop was too high and hence it was as cheap as dirt.

as cheerful as a lark

She is very active and she is as cheerful as a lark.

as clean as a new pin

He keeps his cycle as clean as a new pin.

as curious as a fish

Children show lot of interest in films; they are as curious as a fish.

as cunning as a fox

The manager of that company is as cunning as a fox.

as cruel as death

The terrorists are as cruel as death.

as crisp as a new bank note

The potato chips are as crisp as a new bank note.

as crafty as a fox

Don't believe him; he is as crafty as a fox.

as countless as the stars

The lake was full of swans; they were as countless as the stars.

as complacent as a cat

You are very much selfish, as complacent as a cat.

as common as dirt

The mobile phones have become as common as dirt.

as cold as ice

The window grill has become as cold as ice.

as clear as crystal

Filtered water in the laboratory was as clear as crystal.

as devoted as a faithful dog

You are lucky to have a devoted servant, as devoted as a faithful dog.

as deep as the ocean

I could not see the bottom of the valley; it was as deep as the ocean.

as dumb as a statue

She cannot hear; she is as dumb as a statue.

as dry as dust

The wound on her wrist dried up. It was as dry as dust.

as drunk as a fish

He came late at night; he was as drunk as a fish.

as dirty as ditch water

Due to a breakdown in the filtering plant we got dirty water; as dirty as ditch water.

as eager as a bridegroom

He is waiting for the IAS result; as eager as a bridegroom.

as easy as ABC

The English paper was as easy as ABC.

as empty as space

Believe me; the box is as empty as space.

as fair as the moon

The girl is fair in colour; as fair as the moon.

as faithful as a dog

His servant is very honest and as faithful as a dog.

as fresh as dew

Look at the fresh flowers; they as fresh as dew.

as free as the air

My exam is over and I am as free as the air.

as flat as a billiard table

The site for our house is as flat as a billiard table.

as fit as a fiddle

Keep yourself as fit as a fiddle to take part in sports.

as firm as a rock

My decision is firm, as firm as a rock.

as fierce as a tiger

Tipu Sultan was a great warrior; in the battlefield he was as fierce as a tiger.

as fickle as the weather

She is a fickle minded woman; as fickle as the weather.

as fat as a pig

See that fat guy in theatre; he is as fat as a pig.

as fast as the light

The leopard runs as fast as the light.

as gaudy as a butterfly

She wore a colourful gaudy frock; as gaudy as a butterfly.

as generous as a lord

He has generously donated to many schools; he is as generous as a lord.

as grim as death

The sad news made him grim and gloomy, as grim as death.

as green as grass

The uniform of army soldiers is as green as grass.

as greedy as a dog

The shopkeeper is very greedy, as greedy as a dog.

as grave as a judge

I saw him in a serious mood; he was looking as grave as a judge.

as gracious as the moon

She is very much gracious, as gracious as the moon.

as graceful as a swan

The woman in a pink dress looks attractive and graceful; as graceful as a swan.

as good as gold

The quality of woolen suiting is excellent; as good as gold.

as glorious as the sun

The reign of King Ashok was glorious, as glorious as the sun.

as happy as a child

He is meeting his mother after a long time and he is as happy as a child.

as hungry as a church mouse

I could not take my breakfast today and now I am as hungry as a church mouse.

as hot as fire

The water in the electrical heater is as hot as fire.

as hoarse as a crow

I heard him speak on phone; his voice is as hoarse as a crow.

as helpless as a babe

The thief picked up his purse; his condition was as helpless as a babe.

as heavy as lead

The unattended luggage on the railway platform was as heavy as lead.

as hard as marble

The cement used in the wall is of the best quality and hence it is as hard as marble.

as harmless as a dove

The policeman on duty is as harmless as a dove.

as hateful as hell

Some English officers were hateful towards Indians; as hateful as hell.

as ignorant as a child

He is as ignorant of the facts as a child.

as immortal as the stars

The memory of the freedom fighters has remained as immortal as the stars.

as impatient as a lover

The children were as impatient as a lover to board the plane.

as industrious as an ant

Scientists are as industrious as an ant.

as inevitable as death

Their fight for the ancestral property is as inevitable as death.

as innocent as a lamb

I know him personally; he is as innocent as a lamb.

as lasting as the pyramids

The newly built bridge is as lasting as pyramids.

as loud as a thunder

The noise of the stone crusher is very loud; it is as loud as a thunder.

as light as air

Her luggage for the tour is as light as air.

as lean as a skeleton

His friend is as lean as a skeleton.

as merciless as the grave

That moneylender is as merciless as the grave.

as merry as a cricket

The children are as merry as a cricket.

as meek as a dove

The professor is wise and he is as meek as a dove.

as motionless as a corpse

He was lying unconscious; as motionless as a corpse.

as natural as life

The pictures in the painting are as natural as life.

as new as a day

These chocolates are as new as a day.

as nimble as a bee

The judo teacher is active and he is as nimble as a bee.

as noiseless as a shadow

The tiger stood there as noiseless as a shadow.

as obstinate as a mule

The customer was very difficult to convince because he was as obstinate as a mule.

as old as the hills

See that ancient building; it is as old as the hills.

as open as a smile

He is a free and frank person, as open as a smile.

as pale as death

The students saw the tough question paper and went as pale as death.

as peaceful as sleep

The prayer hall was full to capacity but it was as peaceful as sleep.

as playful as a kitten

She was very sportive by nature and she was as playful as a kitten.

as poor as a church mouse

He is very honest and he is as poor as a church mouse.

as pure as a lily

It is a pure gold; it is as pure as a lily.

as proud as a peacock

She is as proud as a peacock because of her beauty.

as pretty as a picture

I found her as pretty as a picture.

as powerful as a lion

The Indian wrestler is as powerful as a lion.

as quick as lightning

The snake was quick in attacking the fox; it was as quick as lightning.

as quiet as a mouse

He saw his father and remained as quiet as a mouse.

as red as blood

The colour of the flowers was as red as blood.

as regular as a clock

They are very punctual; as regular as a clock.

as ripe as a cherry

The mangoes were as ripe as a cherry.

as round as a globe

The oranges in the orchard are as round as globe.

as strong as a horse

If you take milk and almond regularly, you will be as strong as a horse.

as stealthy as a cat

I could see the thief moving as stealthy as a cat.

as spineless as a jellyfish

He is a timid person; as spineless as a jellyfish.

as solid as bricks

He is a bodybuilder having his muscles as solid as bricks.

as soft as butter

The tender skin of a baby is as soft as butter.

as slow as a snail

Her writing speed is as slow as a snail.

as slippery as an ice

it was drizzling and the road was as slippery as an ice.

as sharp as a razor

The rat's teeth are as sharp as a razor.

as sensitive as a compass needle

Young brains are as sensitive as a compass needle.

as stupid as an ass

He is as stupid as an ass.

as sweet as honey

The oranges from Nagpur are as sweet as honey

as swift as an arrow

Commandos are as swift as an arrow while attacking the enemy.

as tender as a bud

New born baby's fingers are as tender as a bud.

Short Story Telling

Read the short stories loudly. Try to understand the meaning. Once it is understood, you practice telling the story. Tell it to your friends, family members. If nobody is there to listen, stand before the mirror and tell the story to yourself. Remember to tell the story loudly and clearly.

THE CLEVER FOX

Once upon a time, there lived a clever fox. One day he felt very hungry. He roamed about in search of food. By chance, he looked up at a tree. He saw a crow with a piece of meat in its beak. He was pleased to see the piece of meat. But alas! He was unable to climb up the tree. He thought for a moment and made a plan.

He began to praise its black feathers. He said, "My dear friend, what a sweet voice you have! Please sing me a song". The expected thing happened. The foolish crow was highly pleased. It opened its beak to sing. As it did so, the piece of meat fell down on the ground. The clever fox picked it up and walked away happily.

THE CLEVER CROW

One hot day, a crow was dying of thirst. It flew about in search of water. It could not find water anywhere. At last, it saw a jug in a garden. It at once flew to see if there is water in it. It looked in and found that there was a little water in it. It tried hard to reach the water. It then pushed the jug over but it was too heavy to do so. It saw some pebbles lying near the jug.

He thought of a good plan. He then picked up the pebbles one by one and dropped them into the jug. This made the water to rise higher and higher. At last, the water rose to the top. Thus the crow was able to drink the water and satisfy the thirst.

THE LION AND THE RAT

One hot summer day, a lion was sleeping under a tree in the forest. A little rat happened to pass that way. It ran across the body of lion and woke him up. The lion got very angry and caught the rat with its paw. The lion was about to kill the rat. In the meantime, the rat began to beg for mercy. It said, "Oh King of the forest, forgive me and spare my life. I might be able to help you some day in future". The lion laughed and let the rat go.

Some days later, the same lion was caught in a hunter's net. He tried hard to free himself. He could not succeed. He began to roar loudly. The rat whose life he had spared, heard his roar. It at once ran to the place where lion was roaring. It began to bite the ropes of the nest with its sharp teeth. In a short time, the lion was free. Both the lion and the rat became happy. They went away thanking each other.

THE FARMER AND HIS SONS

A farmer had four sons. All four were healthy. They wasted their time and energy in quarrelling with each other. They were not listening to the advice of father. They turned a deaf ear to him.

When the farmer was on death bed, he ordered his servants to bring a bundle of dry sticks. Then he called his sons. When they came, he asked them to break the bundle of sticks. All his sons tried their best and none of them could break the bundle.

Then the farmer told them to untie the bundle and break the sticks one by one. When the bundle was untied, the sticks fell apart. Now all were broken easily.

The farmer said, "Look here my sons. Learn a lesson from this experience. United you stand divided you fall".

From that day onwards, the sons never quarrelled.

RICH MAN AND HIS SERVANTS

There was a rich man. He had a number of servants. One day he found his cash box missing. He searched for the missing box but no trace of theft was found.

He was dead sure that no outsider could steal the cash box. His suspicion was upon his servants. But how to catch the thief was the problem for him. At last, he thought of a plan.

He sent for his servants. He gave each one a stick. He said, "The stick of the thief will grow longer by one inch. So, bring your sticks tomorrow for inspection".

The real thief said to himself, "If I cut one inch off the end of stick, tomorrow it will be of the same length as others". So he cut his stick to avoid detection.

On the next day, the rich man inspected the sticks of his servants. The thief's stick was smaller by one inch. Thus the real thief was caught. He admitted his guilt.

ONCE A LIAR ALWAYS A LIAR

Once there lived a shepherd in a village near a forest. He used to graze his flock of sheep. He used to rest under a tree as the sheep grazed on.

One day he thought of cutting a joke with people working in the fields. He cried at the top of his voice, "Wolf! Wolf! Come, help".

The people in the fields heard his shout. They came running with sticks for help. "Where is the wolf?" they asked him. They were very much surprised when the boy only laughed and said, "There is no wolf. I shouted only for fun". The villagers were very much angry for his mischief and they went back.

A week later, a wolf actually came. The frightened boy climbed upon a tree and shouted for help. "Wolf! Wolf! Come, help".

He cried himself hoarse but nobody came for help. The villagers did not want to be fooled again. The wolf killed many a sheep.

THE LAZY DONKEY

A farmer had an ox and a donkey. The ox was hard working. The donkey was lazy.

One noon, the farmer went to a well to wash his muddy feet. He was surprised to see the donkey and the ox talking under a tree. The farmer began hearing their talk hiding behind the tree.

"I am tired of working under the sun every day. I am surprised to see you so healthy and fine. Won't you tell me your secret?" asked the ox politely.

The donkey laughed and said, "You are very innocent, uncle! You must be smart enough to escape from work like me".

"But how do you escape from work?" asked the ox curiously. "Well, I always pretend to be sick when our master makes me work. He leaves me to take rest. That

way, I eat, sleep and enjoy the life", replied the donkey.

The farmer came to know of the donkey's tricks. Next day, he left the ox in its shed and took the donkey to the field. As usual, the donkey pretended to be sick. But the farmer whipped the donkey with a cane and made him work the entire day. Thus the lazy donkey learnt a lesson.

THE RAT WITH SEVEN TAILS

In a village, a male rat and a female rat got married and set up a family. Surprisingly, a rat with seven tails was born to them.

They carefully looked after the baby rat and admitted it in a school. When it joined the school, the rat's classmates began teasing it as a rat with seven tails.

The baby rat angrily came home and told its mother that his friends were making fun of its extra tails. So the mother rat took it to a tailor and got one of its tails cut. The next day, it went to school and his classmates teased him once again as a rat with six tails. The rat came home again and cried. The mother again took him to the tailor and got another tail removed.

Then they teased the rat as a five tailed rat. This went on till the rat got all its extra tails removed by the tailor. But the teasing did not stop there. The rat was teased for losing all its extra tails foolishly.

Thus there was no end to teasing and the baby rat learnt a lesson of not taking others' teases seriously.

THE BOASTFUL FROG

Once there was an arrogant frog. It used to boast about itself that it knew everything. One day, while the frog

was standing on the river bank, a small fish swam that way. The frog croaked loudly, "Hey fish! Why did you come here without taking my permission?"

The fish was frightened because nobody had spoken to it so rudely. It began to swim towards the other side. But the frog was angry and began to swim along with the fish. It said, "Hey fish! I can live on both land as well as water. But you can't survive on land." The fish did not respond.

"Hey fish! Don't you even know how to speak? Look how fluently I am speaking", said the boastful frog. Even the other fish heard these words but they couldn't speak anything.

Once again to irritate the fish, the frog said, "Hey fish! I am the king. If you don't hop on land along with me, I will kill you." The fish was frightened and followed the frog towards land.

"Now listen to my beautiful song", said the frog and began singing. A snake that was sleeping nearby was disturbed due to its singing. "Who has disturbed my sleep?" asked the snake. It looked around and saw the singing frog and it swallowed the frog. The fish were happy to get rid of the boastful frog.

Introducing Yourself

[Read aloud]

I am Thomas Pinto.

I come from Pune in Maharashtra state.

I have passed M.A. in English securing distinction.

I am teaching English in the government college. Apart from doing M.A. in English, I have passed advance English course conducted by British Council.

Since last 5 years, I am working as the head of the department of English. I teach English to final year students.

I like reading English literature and novels.

Besides reading, I am interested in listening to old film songs. I regularly write for the various magazines and periodicals in English.

I like to watch the game of cricket.

I like to talk to people from different fields.

I like to go on a long drive by car,

INTRODUCING ANOITHER PERSON

[Ashok takes his friend Ramesh to his house and introduces him to his father.]

Ashok	:	Ramesh meet my daddy. Daddy, this is Ramesh, my best friend. He is an automobile engineer.
Father	:	Hello, Ramesh! I am pleased to see you. I hear a lot about you.
Ramesh	:	Hi, Uncle! It is my pleasure to meet you.
Ashok	:	My daddy is in the export business of diamonds. He is always on foreign tour.
Father	:	Ramesh, please feel at home. Stay for lunch with us.
Ramesh	:	Thank you for the invitation but I have to go for an urgent work.
Ashok	:	Daddy, I will take him to a hotel for dinner.
Father	:	What is your father doing?
Ramesh	:	My father is a retired Police Commissioner.
Father	:	Convey my regards to him. Please ask him to visit me whenever he is free.
Ramesh	:	Sure, he will be happy to see you.
Father	:	Ashok. Why don't you offer him a glass of juice?
Ramesh	:	By the way, Ashok, where is your mother?
Ashok	:	Oh! I forgot to tell you. She has gone on a tour of Europe. She will return shortly.
Ramesh	:	Kindly convey my regards to her. I will leave now.
Ashok	:	Let me take you to the bus stop.
Ramesh	:	Hurry up!

ACCEPTING AN INVITATION

[Sameer invites his friend Mohan to his birthday party. Mohan happily accepts the invitation.]

Sameer : Hi Mohan! I came to you in the morning. Your house was locked. Where were you?

Mohan : I was busy in the office for an urgent work.

Sameer : I have come to invite you for my birthday party.

Mohan : Really, when is it? I simply love to attend the party.

Sameer : Don't you remember? Day after tomorrow is my birthday. I have planned for a stag party. I request you to spare your time.

[stag party = party for bachelors]

Mohan : What time is the party?

Sameer : Seven O'clock in the evening.

Mohan : Thank you for the invitation. I would be there at sharp seven.

Sameer : Please come a little earlier. I need your help in the arrangements.

Mohan : Sure! I will be well before the time.

Sameer : Let me take leave. I have to invite many of my friends.

Mohan : Fine! Bye!

NOT ACCEPTING AN INVITATION

[Raman invites his friend Vasu for his son's marriage but Vasu is unable to attend. See how he excuses himself.]

Raman : (on the phone) Hello Vasu, Raman speaking here.

Vasu : Hi Raman, what is the matter? Hope everything is all right.

Raman : I am calling to give you the happy news.

Vasu : What is the news? Tell me, I am eager to listen.

Raman : My son Hari is getting married. I am inviting you.

Vasu : When is the marriage to take place?

Raman : On 9th March, this year.

Vasu : Congratulations! But you have not informed me of the marriage negotiations.

Raman : Believe me, all the things about the marriage were settled in such a hurry that I hardly had any time to consult anybody. Even I could not inform my sisters also.

Vasu : Never mind. It happens like this many times.

Raman : I have sent the marriage card by post. There is no time for coming to call you personally. Please do come.

Vasu : Thank you very much for your invitation. I am afraid I will not be able to attend. I am really sorry about it.

Raman : Why? Are you angry with me?

Vasu : Nonsense! How can you think like that? My daughter is coming from London on 9th morning. I have to go to receive her. I hope you will appreciate my limitation and excuse me for not coming.

Raman : I do realize your stand but I will miss you.

Vasu : Tell my best wishes to your son and daughter-in-law.

Raman : Do remember me to your daughter. Try to come later to bless the newly married couple.

Vasu : Certainly! I will come with my wife.

Raman : All the best! Good day!

Vasu : Bye! Good day!

TAKING LEAVE OF SOMEBODY

[Rekha and Radha are friends. They have been talking to each other for more than an hour and now Rekha wants to take leave of her.]

Rekha : Well, Radha, do you know we have been talking for nearly an hour. I must leave now. I am expecting some guests at home.

Radha : Who is coming to your house?

Rekha : A family is coming to see me for my marriage with their boy.

Radha : Is it so? What is he? How is he?

Rekha : I have not seen him. I know he is an engineer in Mumbai.

Radha : I am so thrilled to know it. I wish you all the best. Please leave.

Rekha : I will see you tomorrow evening.

Radha : Do tell me about the boy. Bye!

Rekha : Bye!

AT THE HOTEL

Avinash : Excuse me! Can I get a room please?

Manager : Yes, of course! Do you want a single room or a double room? And do you want AC or without AC?

Avinash : I need a double room. My wife is also with me.

Manager : Just a minute, please. Let me check up. Sir, at the moment we have only one double room without AC. It is on the fifth floor. It is very calm and quiet.

Moreover, you will get the fresh air all the time.

Avinash : I want a double room with AC on the ground floor. How can you help me?

Manager : Sir, if you don't mind you can occupy the room on the fifth floor now. I will shift you to ground floor later. The lady occupying the room is checking out in the evening.

Avinash : That's fine! Thank you. What is the tariff like?

Manager : Rs. 4000/- per day for double bed room with AC and Rs. 3000/- per day for the double bed room without AC.

Avinash : Is the lift running for 24 hours? Is there room service?

Manager : You don't have to worry sir. We provide room service all the 24 hours and the lift is running round the clock.

Avinash : What other facilities do you provide?

Manager : We organize conducted tours thrice a week to show the places of interest in and around the city.

Avinash : Excellent! Please help me to get my luggage into the room.

Manager : Please sign in the register and go to your room. Your luggage will follow.

TELLING THE TIME

Rajani : Ram, what is the time by your watch? My watch is not running.

Ram : It is quarter-past nine.

Rajani : Any idea what time is our train to Delhi?

Ram : It is at half- past ten.

Rajani : When will it reach Agra?

Ram : It will reach at quarter to five.

Rajani : By the way, when is our connecting train to Jabalpur?

Ram : I think there is an express train at ten past five from Agra. It reaches Jabalpur at five to twelve.

Rajani : Then there is plenty of time. Shall we go to canteen for lunch?

Ram : I also think so. After lunch we can have a little rest in waiting hall.

Rajani : It is a nice idea. I am tired. I need rest.

Ram : OK! Let us go to have lunch quickly.

GIVING A MESSAGE ON PHONE

Rita : Hello, is it 4534442?

Neeta : Yes. May I know who is calling?

Rita : This is Rita.

Neeta : Hi Rita! Whom do you want?

Rita : Can I speak to Reema please?

Neeta : She isn't in right now.

Rita : When is she likely to be back?

Neeta : No idea. She didn't tell me where she was going and what time she would return.

Rita : In that case, would you please pass on a message to her?

Neeta : Yes, of course! Tell me what is it?

Rita : Please tell her that our General Manager would like to see her tomorrow morning at 11 in his office.

Neeta : In what connection?

Rita : Well, she has applied for a job in our company. He has called her for an interview. Give this message to her without fail.

Neeta : Don't worry. I will pass on the message to her personally.

Rita : Thank you very much.

Neeta : Bye!

MEETING AFTER A LONG TIME

Malini : Hello Shalini, how are you?

Shalini : Fine! Thanks and you?

Malini : I am fine too. I have not seen you for ages. Had you been away?

Shalini : No. I was very much here. I was busy in my studies.

Malini : Is it over?

Shalini : It is all over. I have given the exam also.

Malini : I can make out from your face. You look very much relaxed.

Shalini : Though I was busy in my studies. I missed you a lot.

Malini : I also missed you. Anyway I have to attend my class now. Let me go.

Shalini : Do come to my home with free time.

Malini : Certainly! I will come. Bye!

Shalini : Bye!

Words - English and American

The English language is made easier in USA by simplifying the spelling of following words. Study the words for your knowledge.

UK	USA
amoeba	ameba

[a single celled organism that can change shape]

anaemia	anemia

[shortage of red cells in blood]

aesthete	esthete

[a person who appreciates art and beauty]

aeon	eon

[an extremely long period of time]

arbour	arbor

[a shady place in garden with climbing plants]

ardour	ardor

[enthusiasm or passion]

armour	armor

[tough metal to protect the body in battle]

armoury	armory

[a store of weapons]

artefact	artifact

[a man-made object]

UK	USA
baulk [hesitate to accept]	balk
cauldron [a large metallic cooking pot]	caldron
caulk [a waterproof material for filling cracks or joints]	calk
candour [frankness]	candor
Centilitre [a 100th of a litre]	centiliter
centre [a point in the middle of something]	center
cosy [comfortable]	cozy
defence [the act of protecting]	defense
disfavour [dislike]	disfavor
dishevelled [untidy]	disheveled
dishonour [a state of shame]	dishonor

UK	USA
dishonourable [bringing shame]	dishonorable
disc [a flat, thin, round object]	disk
dolour [great sorrow]	dolor
draughtsman [a person who makes technical drawings]	draftsman
oedema [excess fluid in the tissues of body]	edema
endeavour [try hard to achieve something]	endeavor
enthral [fascinate and hold the attention of]	enthrall
epicentre [the place of origin of earthquake]	epicenter
oestrogen [a harmone in female]	estrogen
oesophagus [tube connecting throat to stomach]	esophagus
faggot [a bundle of sticks]	fagot

UK	**USA**
favourite [preferred to all others]	favorite
favourable [expressing agreement]	favorable
favouritism [partial treatment]	favoritism
faeces [excrement]	feces
fervour [passionatefeeling]	fervor
fibre [a strand from a plant or animal tissue]	fiber
flavour [the distinctive taste of a food or drink]	flavor
gauge [an instrument for measuring the pressure]	gage
glamour [an attractive and exciting quality]	glamor
glycerine [a thick sweet liquid used in medicine]	glycerin
grey [a colour between black and white]	gray

UK	**USA**
Instil	Instill
[gradually establish in someone's mind]	
gibe or jibe	gybe
[an insulting remark]	
kilometre	kilometer
[1000 metres]	
labour	labor
[work]	
Labourer	laborer
[worker]	
lacklustre	lackluster
[lacking energy or inspiration]	
liquorice	licorice
[a black substance used as a sweet medicine]	
litre	liter
[1000 millilitre]	
mitre	miter
[a bishop's pointed headdress]	
mould	mold
[a container in which a liquid is poured]	
moulder	molder
[decay]	

UK	**USA**
naevus [a birth mark]	nevus
orthopaedics [branch of medicine about bones]	orthopedics
pyjamas [a jacket or loose trousers for sleeping in]	pajamas
palaeography [study of ancient writings]	paleography
palaeolithic [of the early phase of stone age]	Paleolithic
palaeontology [study of fossil animals and plants]	paleontology
paralyse [affect with paralysis]	paralyze
parlour [a sitting room]	parlor
practise [do repeatedly to improve one's skill]	practice
prize [a thing given to a winner]	prise
programme [a planned series of events]	program

UK	USA
Programming [arrange a series of events]	programing
Psychoanalyse [treat using psychoanalysis]	psychoanalyze
pummelling [striking repeatedly with the fists]	pummeling
rancour [bitter feeling]	rancor
remould [mould again]	remold
revelling [enjoy yourself in a lively way]	reveling
rivalling [competing with others]	rivaling
rumour [spreading of false story]	rumor
sabre [a curved sword]	saber
savour [enjoy the taste of food]	savor
savoury [salty or spicy rather than sweet]	savory

UK	USA
sceptic [doubtful person]	skeptic
sceptre [a staff carried by monarch]	scepter
shrivelling [shrink due to loss of moisture]	shriveling
skilful [having skill]	skillful
snivelling [complaining in a whining way]	sniveling
sombre [dark and gloomy]	somber
spectre [[a ghost]	specter
sulphate [a salt of sulfuric acid]	sulfate
sulphur [a yellow non-metallic element]	sulfur
toxaemia [blood poisoning]	toxemia
tranquillizer [a drug used to reduce tension]	tranquilizer

UK	**USA**
travelling	traveling
[go from one place to another]	
traveller	traveler
[a person who travels]	
tumour	tumor
[abnormal growth of tissue]	
tyre	tire
[rubber covering around a wheel]	
unrivalled	unrivaled
[greater or better than all others]	
unsavoury	unsavory
[unpleasant to taste]	
valour	valor
[bravery]	
wilful	willful
[intentional]	
Woollen	woolen
[made of wool]	

Words Showing Collection

In English language, there are a variety of words indicating a group or collection of persons, animals and things. The knowledge of these words is useful while speaking. Observe carefully, read loudly and try to use in your speech.

An **album** of photos, stamps
She has **an album of photos** taken at the time of her marriage.

An **army** of soldiers
India is having **an army of soldiers** to protect the country.

A **band** of musicians, robbers
An orchestra comprises of **a band of musicians**.
A band of robbers broke open the bank and looted the cash.

A **bale** of cotton, wool
India exports thousands of **bales of cotton** to USA.
Russia imports plenty of **bales of wool** from India.

A **battalion** of soldiers
A battalion of soldiers was deployed along the border to check the smuggling.

A **battery** of guns
To counter the attack on the western border a battery of guns was placed.

A **brood** of chickens
A vulture attacked **a brood of chickens** for its food.

A **bench** of judges
The fast track court is having **a bench of judges** to clear the cases.

A **bevy** of servants
In the olden days, kings were having **a bevy of servants** at their command.

A **block** of flats
Housing societies consist of **a block of** residential **flats.**

A **board** of directors
A board of directors is responsible for running the company.

A **banquet** of flowers
The chief guest was welcomed by **a banquet of flowers.**

A **concourse** of people
Our prime minister was welcomed by **a concourse of people.**

A **bunch** of flowers, grapes, keys
She has arranged **a** beautiful **bunch of flowers** in the pot.
Her mother gave me **a bunch of grapes** for eating.
I lost **a bunch of keys** somewhere on the way to office.

A **catch** of fishes
Fishermen got **a catch of fishes** in the deep sea.

A **bundle** of clothes, hay, sticks
She carried **a bundle of clothes** for washing.

A farmer keeps **a bundle of hay** to feed the cattle.
It is not possible to break **a bundle of sticks**.

A **caravan** of merchants, pilgrims
In the olden days, **a caravan of merchants** was travelling to sell the goods.

A caravan of pilgrims goes on foot to temple far away.

A **chain** of events, mountains

The world war was followed by **a chain of events.**

Himalaya is a large chain of mountains in the northern front.

A **choir** of singers

A choir of singers was present to sing devotional songs.

A **carillon** of bells

A melodious sound of ringing was from **a carillon of bells** in the temple.

A **class** of students

The teacher was giving lecture to **a class of students**.

A **cloud** of locusts

Entire standing crop was eaten away by **a cloud of locusts.**

A **clump** of trees

The fire broke out in the jungle and burnt **a clump of trees.**

A **code** of laws

There was a strong demand for **a code of laws** to stop rape cases.

A **congress** of delegates

The non-alignment conference was attended by **a congress of delegates.**

A **consignment** of goods

We have received **a consignment** of military **goods** from Europe.

A **constellation** of stars

Indian almanac is based on **a constellation of stars**.

A **council** of advisers

Emperor Akbar appointed **a council of advisers** for efficient administration of empire.

A **course** of events

The fall of government was due to **a course of events** not in favour of it.

A **fall** of leaves, snow, rain

Generally **a fall of leaves** is observed in winter.

People in Himalayan range stay indoors during **a fall of snow.**

A fall of rain is necessary for the growth of trees in jungle.

A **fleet** of cars

The company is having **a fleet of cars** for all officers.

A **flock** of sheep

A shepherd tames a couple of dogs to keep the wolf away from **a flock of sheep**.

A **flight** of bees, birds, insects, locusts, steps

The woodcutter was attacked by **a flight of bees**.

I saw **a flight of birds** flying at high altitude.

Entire crop was damaged by **a flight of insects.**

Government is worried of the loss of crop due to **a flight of locusts.**

He was so happy that he covered **a flight of steps** in seconds.

A **flotilla** of boats, ships

Indian Navy has deployed a flotilla of ships in the Indian Ocean.

A **galaxy** of stars, beauties

A galaxy of stars is the combination of millions of planets and stars in space.

A galaxy of beauties attended the international film festival.

A **gallery** of paintings
My friends have planned a visit to Albert hall to see **a gallery of paintings.**

A **gang** of thieves, robbers, workmen
The police arrested **a gang of thieves** trying to break open a bank.
People are scary of **a gang of robbers** looting at midnight.
A gang of workmen was seen laying the railway track on the new route.

A **garland** of flowers
Party workers offered **a garland of flowers** to their leader as a mark of respect.

A **grove** of trees
That bus is having a regular stop near **a grove of** mango **trees** on the highway.

A **heap** of sand, stones
The children were playing on **a heap of sand** in the garden.
A heap of stones was dumped on the roadside for repairing the road.

A **herd** of cattle, deer
You can see **a herd of cattle** grazing beside the river.
A herd of deer can be seen in the jungle.

A **hoard** of gold, jewels
A hoard of gold was found in the cellar of a temple.
The police have caught a smuggler with **a hoard of jewels.**

A **league** of nations
International leaders formed **a league of nations** to avoid war in future.

A **library** of books
The university has **a** huge **library of books** on various subjects.

A **multitude** of people
The prime minister's meeting was attended by **a multitude of people**.

A **muster** of peacocks
I saw a muster of peacocks while passing through the forest.

An **orchestra** of musicians
An orchestra of musicians was engaged to entertain people.

A **pack** of asses, playing cards, wolves
The potter engages **a pack of asses** to carry the clay to his place of work.

For every game, **a** new **pack of playing cards** is used in clubs.

A tiger is always followed by **a pack of wolves** to eat the left-over flesh.

A **panel** of judges

Normally **a panel of judges** attends to cases in the court of law.

A **posse** of constables
A posse of constables was deployed to control the mob.

A **posy** of flowers
She bought **a posy of flowers** for visiting a patient.

A **pile** of arms, bricks, stones, wood
Police found **a pile of arms** in the cellar of a house.
A pile of bricks is used to build a house.
The dog was sleeping over **a pile of stones**.

A pile of wood was taken to saw mill for cutting.

A **queue** of people
There was **a long queue of people** to see the exhibition of handicrafts.

A **range** of hills, mountains
Our village is surrounded by **a range of hills.**
Western India has **a range of mountains** called Sahyadri.

A **rope** of pearls
The king was pleased to gift **a rope of pearls** to a dancer.
A **row** of chairs

A row of chairs was placed before the stage for VIPs.

A **school** of whales
Divers saw **a school of whales** down below the ocean.

A **series** of events
A series of undesirable **events** lead to the dispute.

A **set** of tools
A carpenter needs **a set of tools** for making furniture.

A **sheaf** of arrows
In the olden days, warriors used to carry **a sheaf of arrows** for shooting.

A **shoal** of fishes
Tourists saw **a shoal of fishes** through the transparent base of the boat.

A **shower** of arrows, bullets, rain, stones
Arjun shot **a shower of arrows** to kill Karna in Mahabharat war.
The enemy could not face **a shower of bullets** and ran away from their post.
She was fully drenched by **a** sudden **shower of rain.**

The striking workmen threw **a shower of stones** on policemen.

A **squad** of soldiers
A squad of soldiers was called to shoot all the war criminals.

A **squadron** of ships
The Navy chief ordered **a squadron of ships** to be ready for attack.

A **stock** of goods
Merchants keep **a stock of goods** in warehouse for selling in future.

A **stack** arms, corn, hay, wood
Policemen unearthed **a huge stack of arms** from a terrorist hideout.
Government keeps **a large stack of corn** in warehouses for distribution.
The farmer keeps **a stack of hay** for his cattle.

The trader stored **a stack of wood** for sale.
A **staff** of servants, teachers, officers
There was **a staff of servants** in the royal kitchen.
The school has to engage **a staff of** good **teachers**.
We have **a staff of officers** to tackle any problem.